Thanks you
for your support
Tristan

GW00992229

Furniture
FOR THE
FUTURE

Tristan Titeux

Published by Tristan Titeux Publications,
162 Ladbroke Grove, London, W10 5NA, UK.

ISBN: 978-0-9927509-0-9

A CIP catalogue record for this book is available from the British
Library.

Design by Beth Snowden www.sixeight.co.uk
Editorial Services by The Write Factor
Cover photo by Stefan Lubo www.stefanlubo.com

Acknowledgements

To my beautiful, amazing children – Taro, Lucas, Milo and my new daughter – I love you very, very much and I want you to believe in yourself: to know that you are special and that what you care and think about is special. Don't let anybody put you down – they will do so out of jealousy and self-protection. Don't let your fears stand in front of your dreams: do what you want to do as long as it is good and doesn't harm others – and don't do what anyone else wants you to do. You have a very special gift of life, so make the most of it. Don't waste it, don't be bored and waste your time as a teenager – you will wish you had the time to be bored as an adult! Do something with every minute of your life: read, learn, but also very importantly, part of that is to relax and give yourself time to think and be calm. Don't worry if you don't know what to do with your life, just do as many different things as you can. When you are older it will become obvious what you really want to do if it hasn't already come to you.

Thank you Sarah for being patient with me, for letting me do what I want to do and for giving me four amazing children and for looking after them.

Thank you dad for teaching me discipline, teaching me to not waste my free time, for encouraging me to read and learn, and for showing me I should be proud to be different and not follow everyone else.

Thank you to my sister Cybele for the very valuable help you are giving me to be able to make my dreams come true. I could not do this without you.

To my sister Lucy – thank you for being kind and being there when I was little to take us out to discover the world. I remember all our trips very much.

Thank you mum for supporting me in whatever I wanted to do in life.

Thank you Laura for helping me with the book.

Thank you to all who have contributed to this book.

Foreword

All too often we know very little about the furniture and objects that we buy and use every-day. Tristan's book explores the reasons why we should care and what the implications of our uninformed choices really are. It's a personal story which I'm sure will resonate with many of us — its an engaging and accessible read. But more than that Furniture for the Future inspires us with case studies and examples of a growing group of designers who are prepared to do things better, creating emotive products that excite and stimulate. Tristan is very much part of this movement — demonstrating how to put the wider issues into the context of our lives in a practical, tangible and beautiful way through his own design ethos and furniture production.

Whether you are a designer or consumer, this book will inspire you to think in a way that puts tomorrow's world into your actions today.

- Oliver Heath, Sustainable Architectural & Interior Designer, Writer and TV Presenter

Read more about Oliver on his web-site www.oliverheath.com

Reviews

Furniture for the Future is probably a bit more of a read than you bargained for. It's a bit like shopping for a dining table and chairs, then finding the beautiful house for it to sit in comes with it. The pages are ensconced in his heartfelt passion and their content is layered with enormous depth. It touches on many aspects of consumerism from such a great height, that one might traverse the early chapters feeling ineffectual, as you realise we are all fighting a relentless tide that washes up yet another delivery of product and stuff. However, that passes and aspiration replaces any apathy that was trying to creep in, and it's done in a way that intertwines Tristan's core beliefs with the reality of the wider world. It is thankfully peppered with personal minutiae, which keeps the human element at the very centre of the book.

I've read many books about sustainability and consumerism, but none that call out from the page like his does. It is bang up to date with news of the latest innovations in manufacturing and recycling and Tristan has woven the dark history of what the unenlightened ones did before us and indeed, what the enlightened and negligent ones did after that.

Tristan's optimistic view of how we could continue to produce goods but with a lighter cost to the planet is admirable and his conviction and confidence makes you want to believe it could be true.

The literary quotes and breathtaking imagery that lace all of this convincing narrative together, simply reinforce the messages so many of us already have ingrained in our souls. However, it is the big decision-makers of the world, the heads of industry, the CEOs of the conglomerates that decide the future of our fate, who need to heed the words that Tristan has so eloquently laid out in Furniture for the Future. His book could be the crucial messenger.

Tristan's understanding of the way the media perceive sustainability is probably right; it does tend to be transfixed on the negative: but his book is filled with implementable solutions for a less polluted future that doesn't leave us all champing at the bit to repopulate a new planet. This book exposes the reader to that wider viewpoint, possibly for the first time and it can only leave them with open eyes and with the blood of activism coursing through their veins.

-- Tracey West, author of Book of Rubbish Ideas, poet and broadcaster
http://bookofrubbishideas.wordpress.com/author/rubbishauthor/

Tristan Titeux has an all-encompassing passion for sustainability in all areas of life. His book is honest, informative and factual, showing you the thought process behind his Milo range and more. A true labour of love.

-- Sue Jueno, My Green Directory

This is a remarkable book: from the home out to the world and back again! Packed full of interesting facts and quotes, Furniture for the Future is a beautifully-designed treasure-trove of ideas and suggestions to help us live more lightly on the Earth.

-- Herbert Girardet, Co-Founder, World Future Council

CONTENTS

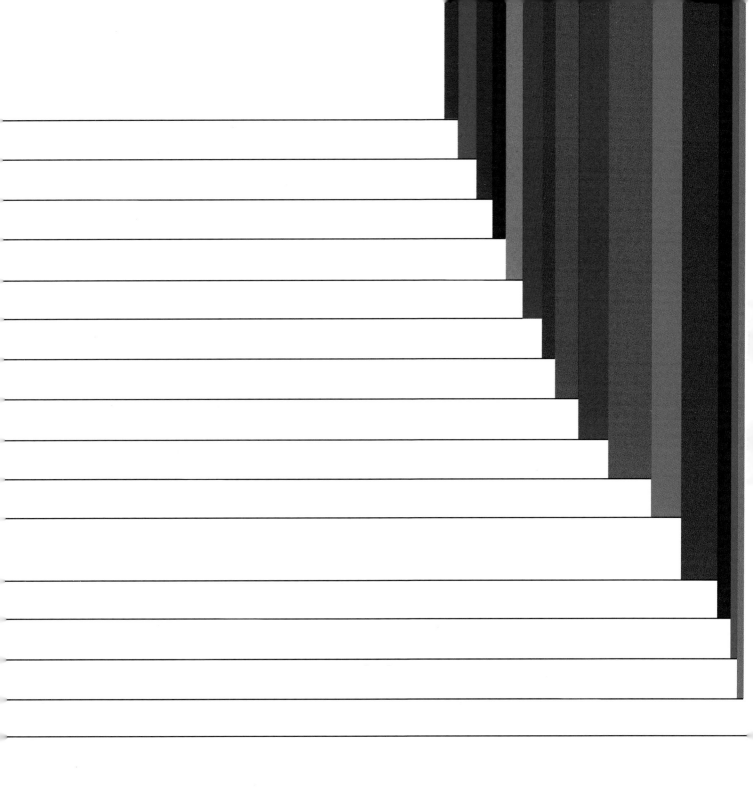

INTRODUCTION: MY STORY

The path to an ecological worldview

I was born in London's Paddington Hospital on 2nd January 1976. I believe a home birth may have been more pleasant for my mum, but I can't honestly say I remember much about it! A few months later we moved to a small, rural village in Belgium called Wonck where my father came from. Wonck is in the Walloon French-speaking area of Belgium, about twenty minutes over the border from Maastricht in Holland. Here started my education at the world famous university of life. My father often said about subjects under discussion that, "one day you will understand," which, as a child, I felt was so patronising. But now with the hindsight afforded by adulthood, I do understand why it is important to be exposed to many and varied experiences as a child.

My childhood was unusual in many ways. We had no TV in the house, but I have no regrets about that as I spent my days playing in the woods or out on my bike. My father was not religious but he taught me to be thankful for everything I have. As a family we all held hands at the dinner table and said the words "Merci pour le repas," (Thank you for the food). I learnt to be grateful for my food and it was nature that we thanked, for she had taken the time to create it for us. As a result of this, I am passionate about food and how it relates to health.

"I believe in God, only I spell it Nature."
Frank Lloyd Wright (1869-1959)

From a young age I came to recognise that nature provides us with not only wonderfully tasting food, but also with effective medicines. I can remember as a child sitting in tears at the dinner table with a bowl of grated horseradish. I had been given it to help remedy a bad cold I was suffering from. It tasted strong, not like children's medicines today, which taste like sweets! I understand now that Mother Nature doesn't sugar-coat her remedies. We used to pick wild chicory – which many people find very bitter – and eat it in our salads, but it is an acquired taste and rather good when dressed in a vinaigrette. Importantly though, it is a great cleansing food, and like many other plants (especially those with yellow flowers) it is a particularly good remedy for kidney or liver problems.

Sometimes you need a greater reason to eat something other than whether or not you find it palatable: sometimes you just need to know that it will make you stronger. I grew up eating healthy, unprocessed food and we were vegetarian for a number of years. My dad loved food too much for this to last forever though, and when I was about ten we gave into temptation and started to indulge in eating meat again. We kept various animals and I grew up watching my mum milk our goats and make cheese from the milk, and I would collect eggs from our chickens. The chickens spent their days happily scratching in the dust and eating grass and bugs. I was never horrified when the animals were killed to provide meat, and have always known that a healthy, happy animal gives healthy meat.

Now that I keep my own chickens I am very conscious that they should lead happy lives, roaming around like the ones I remember from my childhood. I love to see them dust bathing or soaking up the warmth of the sun, but I also know that this lifestyle means that they will provide us with eggs that are higher in Omega-3s and vitamins. According to organic food suppliers Able and Cole, "organic chickens that are reared outside and fed on grass, live longer, healthier lives, have 21% less total fat, 30% less saturated fat and have 50% more vitamin A and 100% more Omega 3 fatty acid."

My parents grew their own fruit and vegetables in the garden and fields around us and they tasted so good, quite unlike those in the supermarkets. The problem with fruit in the shops is that it is picked unripe in order to give it a longer shelf life and the common varieties, produced because they look perfect and uniform, are fast growing and high yielding but this is to the detriment of taste and quality. Nature provides us with different health-giving foods at different times of the year, and by respecting this and consuming foods that are in season, we can get the best health benefits from these. Eating a wide variety of fruits and vegetables can also help to protect us from allergies and diseases.

Our home-grown produce was supplemented with foods bought from the wholefood shops in Maastricht. My mum would take me with her to these shops where the food was unpackaged and unprocessed – the smells were fantastic. My grandmother used to take me to the village bakery where there was a communal oven that the villagers could use to bake their bread and tarts. People shared the oven because they were too poor to afford their own, but this was a great example of how the sharing of resources led to great efficiency and energy conservation. It was a real and very effective community scheme.

The house that we lived in was the oldest in the street, with walls that were 60cm thick and made from flint, stone and chalk. We had a single tap in the whole house. It was in the kitchen and only supplied cold water as there was no boiler or heating system installed. Our heating consisted of a wood burning stove in the kitchen and an open fire in the living room, which meant that in the bitter winters we slept in freezing cold bedrooms. The bathroom was next to the house and the bathwater was boiled in kettles on the stove, so baths were shallow and cold. It was very basic and makes me feel cold just thinking about it! After a bath I would dry off in front of the fire in the living room, and I appreciated the heat that nature provided us. We had selected, gathered and chopped the logs for burning and knew the quantity of wood burned: these were not just units on a meter.

Living like that taught us the true value of things: that water was not to be wasted. We used only what was needed, by not leaving the tap running whilst brushing our teeth, for example. (According to the World Health Organisation, less than 1% of the world's water is readily accessible for direct human use.) Our toilet was some way from the house and overlooked our wonderful garden, so I would always leave the door open and stare out at the beautiful trees and plants, a habit that I have never lost!

The River Meuse flowed past the front of our house but in those days it was used like a sewer. I used to see all sorts of rubbish floating past: the contents of people's bins, bottles, the odd football, even a pig's head! This was in the 1980s but looked more like something from the Middle Ages. Just 50 years before, people had been able to swim, wash their clothes and fish in that river. Thankfully, in the 1990s efforts were made to clean up the river, but I will never forget the sight of that pollution and seeing this waste in the beautiful river had a profound effect on me.

My father, José, was my mentor and was supported closely by my mum. His father, my grandfather, had spent the entirety of World War II as a prisoner of war and so lost out on a good five years of his son's childhood. On his return he imposed a particularly straight and strict Catholic upbringing on him, but my father rejected this way of life as he grew up. My father was inspired by my mum's interest in plants and became an expert in their history and their nutritional and medicinal value. In fact, he became a bit of a horticultural celebrity, appearing on television and having a weekly radio show!

I can remember planting trees with him along the river in front of our house. We just poked long willow sticks into the earth and these grew into trees. I loved the simplicity of it. I used to enjoy mushroom-hunting with my dad too. He knew so much about all the varieties and he taught me to pick them carefully, to respect their surroundings and not to take them all. From a young age my dad also took me on marches and protests. I particularly remember a large anti-nuclear rally in Bruxelles. This opened my eyes to some of the world issues that people were unhappy about.

My father also taught me to fish and we would often go with my uncles. They showed me how to select the right hook and bait for each particular fish. We always caught just enough for our needs and no more. This was sustainable fishing, not the wasteful type that drags up everything in its path with a huge net.

16

Manger sain, manger des plantes sauvages

Sous la quiétude végétale de la vallée du Geer,
le potager de José Titeux est une ode à la nature sauvage

17

"He that planteth a tree is a servant of God; he provideth a kindness for many generations, and faces that he hath not seen shall bless him."
- Henry van Dyke

LE JARDIN EXTRAORDINAIRE DE JOSE TITEUX

POUR AVOIR UN GRAND CHOU, IL FAUT LE CHOUCHOUTER...!

Depuis quelque temps déjà, José Titeux nous a habitué à admirer des légumes hors du commun qu'il récolte dans son jardin.

Cette fois, c'est un chou de plus de 9 kilos qu'il a préparé, un choux bien ferme aux larges feuilles que son fils avait peine à porter. Et, chose importante, qui fut cultivé sans aucun produit chimique.

Quand nous demandons à José comment il fait pour avoir de pareils choux, il nous répond en souriant : « En le chouchoutant, en lui parlant, en l'encourageant à grandir. Et tout en le tapotant gentiment, je lui ai dit... vas-y mon chou ».

Une méthode comme une autre de cultiver et celle-ci démontre à quel point elle est efficace.

19

18

20

21

Photo : Faculté Agronomique de Gembloux.

ZONE VERTE

Le **Pissenlit** (*Taraxacum vulgare* Schrank sensu lato ; famille des Composées). - Cette plante est bien connue de tous ; elle est très commune dans les prairies, les bords de chemin, les terrains vagues... Les capitules jaune d'or sont portés sur des tiges lisses et creuses. A la cassure, il s'échappe, des tiges ou des feuilles, un liquide blanc comme du lait, le latex qui contient du caoutchouc. On ne confondra pas avec le tussilage (fiche n° 12) qui fleurit au premier printemps tandis que la floraison du pissenlit s'étend d'avril à octobre.

22

"Environmentalists have long been fond of saying that the sun is the only safe nuclear reactor, situated as it is, some ninety-three million miles away."
Stephanie Mills, (*In Praise of Nature*, 1990)

23

My great-uncle built a fantastical tower in the village where I lived, complete with one of the Four Horsemen of the Apocalypse on each tower. It was made from unprocessed, uncut flint stone from his quarry. Inside he created beautiful murals and sculptures, a lot of which related to his strong anti-war stance. He was fascinated by history, particularly local history and even spent time digging in local caves for dinosaur fossils. My friends and I would often spend time fossil-hunting in the quarry and found numerous squid and other fossils there. We could literally see the layers of life that had gone before us in the cliff face, and I had a great sense that we were just a miniscule part of the history of the world. When I go back to Belgium now, I always meet up with my friend, a local historian and archaeologist, who has a wealth of knowledge about how people lived in the past. I believe that learning from history can teach us so much about the present and future.

In 1988, in my early teens, I moved to London with my mum, leaving my dad and our rural life in Belgium behind. This was my first experience of town living and I am still in London to this day. At first, I felt quite trapped in the confines of our flat, although I discovered a lot of new things through the medium of TV, watching a lot of nature and cookery programmes. I even enjoyed a little gardening on our roof terrace! Several years later I was fortunate enough to get an allotment but by this time had lost the patience and time required to grow my own food.

24

I carried on learning though, teaching myself about the biodiversity of plants, vegetables and animals. I found out that there are huge varieties of vegetables that are unavailable in the supermarket but that the Heritage Seed Library held a collection of around 800 'heirloom' varieties. I became a member, which has meant that each year since joining I have been able to choose a few packets of heritage seeds for free.

25

26

My bedroom was a big loft room and I converted part of it into a workshop. I used to use the space for building wooden planes or taking things apart to see how they worked: I have always been fascinated by how things are put together. At this time, I studied and got a qualification in Permaculture design. Permaculture is 'the study, planning and implementation of naturally-productive ecosystems for the purpose of creating spaces to live and eat from the provisions of the land.'

I went to college but do not consider myself academic. I have always struggled with words and this book comes more from the heart than an academic perspective, so I am convinced that some greater power must be helping me to write it! I did however study photography and did particularly well in this, enthusiastically reading everything on the subject. I am a very visual person and take pictures of everything. This is another passion of mine, and my way of remembering and appreciating the wonderful things around me.

27

0.1.16

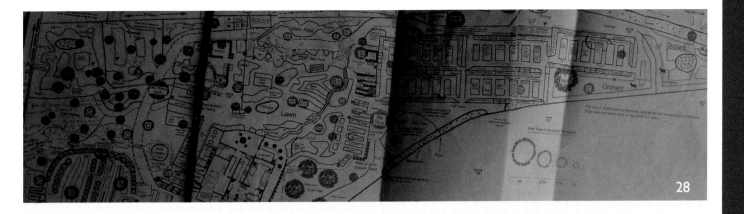

1. The valley where I grew up in Belgium.
2. The whole family with my baby sister and cousin Laura holding the cat.
3. My little sister dicing with death!
4. Me.
5. There was a path that cut straight through a sweetcorn field – that was fun!
6. Having cheese fondue in the Swiss mountains (my older brother was Swiss).
7. My cousin Laura and me outside the barn.
8. I love chickens and after keeping them when I was little I carried this on in adulthood.
9. My sister Cybele holding a friendly chicken.
10. My dad used to love adding wild salad leaves and flowers from the garden to our dinners
11. Another example of flowers and leaves with egg and prawn stuffed tomatoes
12. My sister Cybele and my dad in his office surrounded with the books he used to research wild plants for his radio programme.
13. Special occasion: having diner in the living room in front of the open fire – it must have been the weekend. I can see mussels there, yum!
14. Me in my teenage years picking cherries. We used to go up the valley in the fields and gorge on the best cherries we could find.
15. Family picnic in the fields with my older sister Lucy on the left.
16. Me picking blackberies with my dad at around 2 years old in the local quarry.
17. My dad being filmed for the TV in his garden.
18. Me holding a huge organic cabbage that my dad claimed you have to talk to, to grow this big!
19. My dad photographed by Yvon Hamers.
20. My cousin Laura and me playing on disused quarry truck. We spent a lot of time in the local quarries.
21. A printed card that my dad wrote about wild plants and their uses as part of three packs of around 50 cards.
22. I used to love going picking wild mushrooms with my dad.
23. My dad being filmed.
24. The 'Tour d'Eben-Ezer' built by my great uncle to represent Peace.
25. The tower just after construction.
26. Playing in the caves in the local quarry.
27. I always had a workshop in my various bedrooms. I am soldering something here. I used to build planes and loved taking things apart.
28. I love planning and dreaming: this is a 2-acre Permaculture plan that I created of a plot of land where I hoped to live and grow food and have animals.

1.1

SUSTAINABLE, RENEWABLE, DIVERSE

Defining principles for a healthy planet

Why is sustainability important?

"Sustainable development meets the needs of the present generation without compromising the ability of future generations to meet their own needs."
The Brundland Commission of the United Nations, 1987

The word 'sustainability' comes from the Latin *sustinere* which means to hold up from below. Let me give you an everyday example: a marathon runner needs to drink water for his run to be sustainable. Without it he would get very dehydrated and possibly even die. As for the water itself, it is drunk, passed through the body filtered by nature and is eventually ready to be drunk again. These are two sustainable cycles. Working non-stop is unsustainable because eventually you would die of exhaustion and fatigue. Everyone needs to eat, drink, rest and play.

For a sustainable, healthy life, variety in our diet is of paramount importance. Eating a single food – bread for example – would eventually lead to illness or intolerance. According to the NHS, 1-2 people in every 100 have a food allergy. The number of people with food intolerances is far higher than it used to be, and in many cases results from a lack of variety in our diets. Quite simply modern lifestyles are making people ill, because they are unsustainable.

Good quality homemade bread reduces the likelihood of food intolerances. ▶

With regard to our planetary home, we need to think about sustainability in terms of hundreds of thousands of years to come. Our current lifestyles will adversely impact planetary systems for our children, and our children's children – in fact, way beyond the 'Seventh Generation' which is an Iroquois (native American) timeframe for sustainability. The vast quantity of rubbish tipped into landfills throughout the world, for example, is not a physically maintainable process. These huge tips, which are ever increasing in numbers, are filled with the nastiest chemical cocktails and are causing serious harm to our health and our environment. In 2009, UK residents disposed of more than 14.6 million tonnes of waste into landfill. The Local Government Association estimates that landfill space could run out as soon as 2016. Are we heading in the direction of places like Lagos where numerous people eat, sleep and make their living on rubbish dumps? According to UNICEF over 43,000 children and teenagers work on rubbish dumps in Brazil alone.

This is the inevitable outcome of unsustainable lifestyles where consumer goods are used once and thrown into holes in the ground: in the end we are surrounded by waste and the serious environmental consequences of landfill sites. At long last packaging manufacturers are beginning to address this problem of waste to landfill and are designing products and packaging that can be recycled. It is important to remember that waste is only an abundance of resources in the wrong place – there is no such thing as waste in natural systems as everything is recycled and reused through the processes of death, putrefaction, decomposition and growth.

More worrying than chemicals and plastics in landfill, are the radioactive waste products of nuclear power stations. It is unknown how long this material will take to dissipate safely into nature – perhaps millions or even billions of years. In terms of technology it is amazing that we are capable of producing such power, but I truly believe humanity can invent better forms of power that don't carry deadly waste as a by-product. Nuclear power is unsustainable and dangerous. We need to be looking for other solutions to our energy needs, but for this to happen, political willpower – that is not guided by commercial pressure or internal lobbying – is needed. In Germany in the summer of 2012, for the first time ever 50% of the country's energy needs was generated by solar and wind-power. This goes to show that the dream of sustainable energy can be achieved.

"In its broadest ecological context, economic development is the development of more intensive ways of exploiting the natural environment."
Richard Wilkinson

Nature is surely the ultimate teacher in this subject of sustainability, and we have much to learn from natural cycles. Saint Bernard (1090-1153) said, "You will find something more in woods than in books. Trees and stones will teach you that which you can never learn from masters." A simple example is the cycle of rain falling from the clouds, running down the mountain, into a stream, a river and then the sea and eventually being evaporated and re-forming back into clouds. Other natural cycles are the phases of the moon and the tides which are affected by them, the seasons and a woman's monthly menstrual cycle.

First-nation Americans (or native Indians as they have been known) knew the value of sustainability and cycles in nature – and the dangers of breaking theses sacred systems. In a famous speech, Black Elk, a Holy Man of the Oglala Sioux tribe who lived from 1863 to 1950 said:

"You have noticed that everything an Indian does is in a circle, and that is because the Power of the World always works in circles, and everything tries to be round. In the old days all our power came to us from a Sacred Hoop of the Nation and so long as the hoop was unbroken the people flourished. The flowering tree was the living centre of the hoop, and the circle of the four quarters nourished it. The east gave peace and light, the south gave warmth, the west gave rain and the north with its cold and mighty wind gave strength and endurance. This knowledge came to us from the outer world with our religion. Everything the Power of the World does is done in a circle. The sky is round and I have heard that the earth is round like a ball and so are all the stars. The wind, in its greatest power, whirls. Birds make their nests in circles, for theirs is the same religion as ours. The sun comes forth and goes down again in a circle. The moon does the same and both are round. Even the seasons form a great circle in their changing and always come back again to where they were. The life of a man is a circle from childhood to childhood, and so it is in everything where power moves. Our tepees were round like the nests of birds, and these were always set in a circle, the Nation's Hoop, a nest of many nests, where the Great Spirit meant for us to hatch our children."

What does 'renewable' mean?

Renewable, eco-friendly, natural, free range, organic, ethical, fair trade – these are all words that are now commonly used and are all encompassed in the meaning of the word sustainability. Whilst total sustainability should be the ultimate aim, there are differing degrees of sustainability: things are not always black and white. If chemical fertiliser is used for a short time until a better alternative is found the land will eventually recover, but use chemical fertilisers over and over again and it will result in destructive pollution. The world may not be ready to switch to a sustainable way of life overnight. In the meantime though, it is possible to make the best of the processes that we do use.

Bamboo is a renewable resource that can be grown sustainably. © Christian Degroote ▸

One example is the biodegradable plastic bag that is a by-product of the fossil fuel industry. The downside is that they are made using a finite resource in the form of petroleum; the upside is that they can degrade into something that can be assimilated back into nature. The manufacturers of this plastic say, "D2W converts ordinary plastic at the end of its useful life into a material with a completely different molecular structure. At that stage it is no longer a plastic but has become a material which can be bio-assimilated in the environment in the same way as a leaf." This is a positive way of using a by-product of petrol until a renewable alternative can be found – perhaps from plant or seaweed resources – but preferably not from a food crop. We need our food to eat!

So how renewable are the everyday objects that surround us? Let's take the humble office paper cup. The paper itself is likely to have come from trees but actually could have come from any plant fibre, such as bamboo. These are renewable resources, grown without the use of petrol-derived chemicals. If the energy used in the harvesting process is from a renewable source such as solar or wind power, then this is a relatively clean and renewable system. After they have been used, the cups can be cleaned and re-used, then eventually recycled, composted or burned, making this a low-impact, sustainable process.

The production of plastic office cups is drastically different. Oil is used, which is not only a non-renewable, finite resource, but can potentially cause environmental disasters such as the recent oil spill in the Gulf of Mexico. It takes lots of energy and chemicals to manufacture oil-based products which are then imported vast distances. Using imported petroleum means we are reliant on countries that may not have the same ethics and human rights that we have, and because oil is such a lucrative resource, it is deemed worth fighting wars over. There is little room for diversity in a world that relies so heavily on products that contain petroleum. This 'magic' material is used in everything from clothing to chewing gum, from drugs to carpets to toothbrushes, and obviously to run our cars, heat our homes and power industry.

"Nature provides a free lunch, but only if we control our appetites."

– William Ruckelshaus, Business Week, 18th June 1990

It is crucial that humanity understands the concepts of sustainability and renewability. The way our current manufacturing systems operate is akin to tearing down a forest with a giant digger just to get some mushrooms, when it is obvious that the most appropriate and long-term way to harvest mushrooms is to have people gathering them with baskets, leaving enough to grow back to ensure future harvests.

Medium Density Fibreboard (MDF) wood – that my company uses mostly to make our fitted furniture – falls into the 'not always black and white' category. If we were to use Forest Stewardship Council (FSC) certified wood, which means that it is grown in well-managed forests and harvested responsibly, one would assume that this would be the most sustainable material for eco-furniture. But, there is still some way to go for commercial forests to be truly sustainable. For that to be the case, the forests would need to contain many diverse species and to be left undisturbed for longer to recreate nature's perfect ecosystems. Undoubtedly, wood from commercial forests is much better than cutting down trees from old growth forests and rainforests.

Cross section of old-growth tree. © Dmitriy Karelin ▶

However, with MDF, only the 'thinings' (surplus trees that are cut down to create better light conditions for the remaining trees) from FSC woodlands are used, plus sawdust, a waste product from saw mills. Medite MDF for example uses "local" wood that is grown in Ireland, (local in the sense that it doesn't come from Africa). But now here's the grey area: it uses glues derived from petrochemicals that are not so good for your health. MDF is also difficult to recycle but new technologies are being tested that will enable it to be recycled soon. Currently MDF is not truly sustainable, because of its use of fossil-fuel-derived glues, but it does make use of a waste product from a relatively sustainable system. One of my aims is to raise awareness of MDF's potential to be truly sustainable and to help develop and produce a greener, healthier version of it.

A new material called Tricoya has been invented which, it is claimed, uses a natural manufacturing process to make MDF sawdust waterproof and 100% recyclable. The company already makes Accoya which is a process that transforms pine, a softwood, into a wood that mimics the qualities of hardwood, through a process called 'acetylation' which they describe as similar to steeping conkers in vinegar! It can make a typical plank of pine last for over 80 years outside in the rain without rotting, whereas untreated pine would last maybe 5-10 years at the most. Accoya is an absolutely amazing product, and proof that we are heading in the right direction - towards sustainability!

Architects and the construction industry need to be more aware of such innovative materials and design them into their builds, making their use the norm rather than the exception, otherwise we will be in danger of losing them before they have even served their purpose, or equally worryingly, that a market competitor will buy and bury the patent, like many great inventions in the past. This is no mere sweeping statement: there were 5135 inventions held under secrecy orders in 2010 in the US Patent and Trademark Office. Under the Invention Secrecy Act of 1951 patent applications on new inventions can be subject to secrecy orders restricting their publication if government agencies believe that disclosure would be "detrimental to national security."

The current list of technology areas used to screen patent applications for possible restriction under the Invention Secrecy Act is not publicly available and has been denied under the Freedom of Information Act. But a previous list dated 1971 and obtained by researcher Michael Ravnitsky is available on the internet. Most of the listed technology areas are closely related to military applications, but some of them range more widely. For example the 1971 list indicates that patents for solar photovoltaic generators were subject to review and possible restriction if the photovoltaics were more than 20% efficient. Energy conversion systems were likewise subject to review and possible restriction if they offered conversion efficiencies "in excess of 70-80%".

Hemp: a plant for the future

Hemp is one of many materials I find fascinating, and it has a particularly interesting history. I would like to see hemp being used for all sorts of products and I am promoting its use for making eco-fitted furniture. Years ago, before I started making furniture, I was lucky enough to have a lot of spare time, which I used to study all the positive ideas and inventions that could help to change the world for the better – and hemp is one of them. It has many uses in the building, paper and food industries, but at that time, I was looking into the use of recycled chip fat to make biodiesel, and I was planning on making a business of it, collecting used chip fat and then processing it into a diesel fuel suitable to go straight into any diesel vehicle without modification. I used to have a diesel VW camper van and planned to just pour up to half a tank of this vegetable oil into the vehicle without needing an engine conversion. In the end, for many reasons, I didn't go down that path, but I was inspired by the idea that you are taking someone's waste material and turning it into something to run your car with! Now, even Macdonald's are using the waste cooking oil from their many restaurants to make biodiesel with which to run their fleet of lorries – and in many parts of the countryside, you can smell a local workman's van that is run on cooking fuel as it rumbles past. So the idea is at last catching on.

This is not new technology: the original diesel engine that Rudolph Diesel invented was designed to run on hemp seed oil. Right back in 1894, pollution was an important issue to Diesel who saw his engine as a solution to inefficient, polluting and fuel-wasting coal-powered steam engines. If we had gone along with Diesel's vision, we would now take for granted, a clean renewable oil that is non-toxic, non-flammable, not explosive, easy to store, transport and handle, and when burned, doesn't contribute to the greenhouse effect. In comparison to the 'dirty oil' that causes so much death, destruction and pollution, we have to ask the question – why didn't we stick with renewable, hemp-seed based biodiesels as our fuel? Think how much more advanced we'd be as a civilisation if people had encouraged Rudolph Diesel's invention. Sadly, this was not to be the case.

So what happened? In the late 1920s, William Randolph Hearst, a newspaper man, along with Lammont Dupont of the famous Dupont chemical company, were heavily investing in timber and oil resources and so hemp as a fuel threatened their industries. Over the next few years, a series of patents filed by Dupont and Hearst, together with congressional laws, put paid to the use of hemp in any form in industry: in 1937, the Marijuana Tax Act forbade hemp farming in the US (perhaps deliberately confusing plants that have medicinal and psychoactive properties with *cannabis sativa* which doesn't).

In the same year Dupont filed a patent for nylon, a 'wonder' material made from petroleum. With hemp oils safely out of the way, nylons and synthetic fuels made from petroleum were developed unimpeded. Interestingly, Dupont's major financial backer was Andrew Mellon, the Secretary of State for the Treasury. Together, they were able to push the marijuana prohibition bill through Congress in less than three months, which destroyed the domestic hemp industry in the US.

This is how a handful of people with vested interests were able to stop the use of a raw material that is so beneficial to humanity and the planet. One reason, as alluded to above, is that many people mistake hemp for a drug: whilst there are species in the same genus that do have medicinal properties, cannabis sativa is low in the psychoactive chemical THC (tetrahydrocannabinol). It is time we distinguished once and for all between the two, and reinstated cannabis sativa in its rightful place as a 'Plant for the Future'.

Hemp farming is one of the oldest industries on the planet, dating back more than 10,000 years. The *Columbia History of the World* states that the oldest relic of human history is a bit of hemp fabric dating back to approximately 8,000 BC.

Hemp stalk contains bast fibres which are among the longest and softest natural fibres and are also rich in cellulose.

Marine Hemp Twine Images © *Dreamstime* ▶

Presidents Washington and Jefferson both grew hemp. Americans were legally bound to grow hemp during the Colonial era and early Republic.

The federal government subsidised hemp during World War II and US farmers grew about a million acres of hemp as part of that programme.

Eco-friendly hemp can replace most toxic petrochemical products. Research is being undertaken to use hemp in manufacturing biodegradable plastic products, plant-based cellophane, oils, resins and other products.

Hemp grows well without herbicides, fungicides or pesticides. Almost half of all agrichemicals used in the US are applied to cotton, which hemp makes a great substitute for.

Hemp produces more pulp per acre than timber on a sustainable basis and can be used for every quality of paper.

Hemp fibreboard produced by Washington State University was found to be twice as strong as wood-based fibreboard.

Hemp seed is far more nutritious then soya bean, contains more essential fatty acids than any other source and is second only to soya as a complete protein (but is more digestible by humans). It is high in B-group vitamins and is 35% fibre.

The hydrocarbons in hemp can be processed into a wide range of biomass energy sources, from fuel pellets to liquid fuels and gas.

Hemp seed is not psychoactive and cannot be used as a drug.

Hemp fibre is longer, stronger, more absorbent and more insulative than cotton fibre.

Hemp paper manufacturing can reduce wastewater contamination and its low lignin content reduces the need for acids used in pulping.

Diversity:
the spice of life!

Variety and diversity are key to a successful and happy life: the more experiences you expose yourself to, the more you can learn. As head of a small business I know that the more diverse experiences I encounter, the better overall decisions I make. In everyday health and fitness, undertaking different types of exercises – walking, swimming, cycling – improves overall wellbeing in a balanced way. If you do press-ups and nothing else, you will just get certain muscles becoming bigger but the rest will be neglected, so you need a variety of exercise, from running, cycling, warming up, a few weights, a bit of rowing etc., to get to all the parts in your body as equally as possible.

Solar panels and wind turbines provide a diverse and resilient source of renewable energy. © Esbobeldijk ▶

It is equally important to have a varied diet too – eat all sorts, not just vegetables or tonnes of fruit because you think fruit is the best thing for you – no, it is better to eat a diverse range of different foodstuffs that may include a bit of meat or fish too. That way, your body is getting a full and varied diet that will serve you well. Whatever you do, you need to have diversity.

If ever you hear that someone is offering a solution that will solve everything, you know that it's not likely to be true. The media love to come up with headlines such as "could this be the solution we have been waiting for?" or "finally a solution to end poverty," but in reality, there's no 'one-size-solves-all' solution – just like a healthy varied diet, we need diverse solutions working together to resolve the complex crises we face. Unfortunately there is no magic bullet. Just like there's no miracle medicinal cure for cancer, we need to distrust anyone who says that their solution will save the planet – whether it's through wind power, solar energy or even nuclear power or genetic engineering.

Fortunately, there is a multitude of solutions: we need wind, solar, wave and every other technology working together, guided by local geography, traditions and cultures – and not simply by commercial interests. We must put people and planet before profit. So, we need to combine the right solution, with the right people in the right place: a diverse plan which also includes energy saving and energy reduction; we need to consume less and consume better, (ie: longer-lasting quality); we need to enjoy what we have more and make the most of what we have. We need to turn off lights and machines at night, turn down heating by a couple of degrees, use less packaging, buy produce with less packaging, even use both sides of a piece of paper when you can!

> "Health is not valued
> 'til sickness comes."
> Dr. Thomas Fuller, *Gnomologia*, 1732

A chocolate treat makes many of us very happy, but too much of a good thing can make us sick! All things are best in moderation. ▶

If we choose just one thing thinking it will make us happy or solve a problem, we will get into trouble. We can't just rely on one source for happiness – or anything else for that matter – because if that source is blocked then we are stuck. Diversity truly is the spice of life! If you think eating chocolate will make you happy and so just eat chocolate constantly, it will soon become clear that what you are feeling is the opposite of happiness! It may be part of your solution to overall wellbeing, but you need lots of ways to keep happy and preferably not just from external sources either, or quick fixes such as chocolate! We need diversity: we need it both in quick fixes and in medium and long term fixes, so go and get yourself a nice piece of chocolate! (Ideally Fairtrade, organically grown!)

Diversity keeps disease at bay: in the jungle for example, no one thing can take over and spread disease and eradicate the forest – forest ecosystems encourages diversity to protect itself! The opposite extreme is a monoculture where just one crop is grown: the risk of disease outbreak is much higher and if there is an outbreak it spreads like wildfire and eradicates the whole harvest. The only way to stop it is using nasty polluting and dangerous chemicals to control it.

◀ *Spraying synthetic chemicals on crops destroys pests and diseases, but all the diversity of life too, leaving behind dead soils and toxic residues.* © Antpkr

A diverse landscape evolves natural symbiotic relations with insects and other plants to balance and complement each other. It is never a good idea to just have one crop as in a monoculture or plantation: epidemics start that way. The potato famine is an example of what can happen when you rely on just one product – if disease breaks out and eradicates the crop, when all the population relies on are potatoes to eat, then sadly people starve and die. A healthy environment will not be created with one super-crop: we should not cover the whole country with oil-seed rape for example because though we may think that it will replace oil and so therefore provide a convenient solution to climate change, if that one crop were to fail, we would be in serious trouble, with no biodiesel to fuel our trucks and power stations.

Furniture for the Future by Tristan Titeux

Farmers' Markets and the Living Label

Locally-grown produce on sale at a farmers' market can be tasted before it is bought – just one great reason to shop there. ▼

Let's have another example of diversity, because I love diversity! Many farmers now grow just a few crops for a few companies, or even just one supermarket and are at the mercy of their demands: if the buyers don't like the crop size or colour they could just refuse it and farmers would be in trouble. Many have gone out of business, because they just had one customer. More than 60,000 farmers and farm workers lost their jobs from 1996-2002 in England: the largest exodus of farmers since World War II. But many of those still surviving are diversifying their activities, growing a wider variety of produce, offering additional services, holiday rentals, mountain biking, trekking, fishing, play centres, providing ready-made food and selling a variety of quality products to a wider variety of customers through farm shops and online. Many go to farmers' markets where they can meet their customers face to face, tell them about their produce and how it is grown – they are the living label, the talking label. Now that's an expensive sophisticated technology! A talking label that can explain what something is made of, what breed the beef or pork is.

Farmers' markets are great, I love them – have you been to one? Have a look at www.londonfarmersmarkets. co.uk to find a farmers' market near you. Many items are actually cheaper, especially vegetables and apples, and most are either organic or near to organic compared to the usual supermarket stuff, plus the quality is better. You can get a lot of rare breed meats there that don't taste like the supermarket fare, that are bred for size, fast growth and maximum profit (again a solution that suits the people making money, but not us, the consumers, who want tasty and healthy food).

Farmers' markets have sprung up in the past ten years. The first farmers' market opened in 1997 and now there are over 800 in the UK as well as over a thousand farms shops, which proves that many people who value quality, care very much about where their food comes from and care about healthy food that is not mass-produced. Many of these markets are started by farmers who are diversifying, or by young people who want to offer real healthy quality food and have seen the state of food in supermarkets and wanted to do something about it.

In conclusion, I believe humanity has the potential to invent and create the technologies we need to lead a healthy, sustainable lifestyle. It is possible to recreate our ultimate dreams: well, almost anything is possible, apart from perhaps recreating a human brain with thoughts and feelings, but then again, one day that may happen! How strange we human beings are – we strive to recreate a human being using complex technological means, when all we really need is two consenting adults! Nature knows how do it best!

There is a branch of technology called 'Biomimicry' which looks at how nature approaches design and technology, and implements similar solutions to our own problems. Biomimicry has found out how to make self-cleaning windows using a similar structure to a water lily that grows through the mud at the bottom of a pond. Biomimicry has taught us how to implement better water management systems and more efficient solar cells. If we couple humanity's ingenious, competitive streak with the wisdom of nature, we will be able to create sustainable systems that will lead to an enhanced, healthier and more productive future. However, we have spent the last 150 years burning precious fossil fuels and that has led to climate instability – so time is of the essence. Wisdom and creativity must be harnessed now if we are to have a future.

1.2

DEAD END

Why is humanity taking the path to oblivion?

Humanity is not inherently bad – but we are a highly competitive species that has become the top-predator and the most successful animal of all time. Of course this does depend on how you define successful: humanity – one species among millions on the planet – now consumes so much of the world's available resources that it is out-competing all other species. That is successful in Darwinian terms, but ultimately, if we destroy other forms of life on the planet, we destroy our own ability to survive. We are part of the web of life and all species within that web are co-dependent. We destroy the habitat of bees and insects at our own peril, although to some, it seems of little consequence at the time.

The opposite of sustainability is a dead end and humanity is travelling towards a dead end because our pursuit of economic growth at all costs doesn't take into account (and I mean literally on the spreadsheets of the banks and governments of this world) that once we have destroyed the last tree in pursuit of profit, we will be destitute – even if we have gold aplenty. A healthy planet is the only true wealth, but we have forgotten this as we pursue consumer growth and financial gain. What good is money in the bank if there is nothing to eat?

"The struggle to save the global environment is in one way much more difficult than the struggle to vanquish Hitler; for this time the war is with ourselves. We are the enemy, just as we have only ourselves as allies."
Al Gore

As I said earlier though, humanity is not inherently bad – it is inherently good, but it has lost the path of wisdom, and it fails to listen to its Elders. Our Elders – and by this I mean the remaining indigenous cultures who still live in harmony with nature – know that what we do to the Earth we do to ourselves. They know cutting down diverse rainforests to produce a monoculture of soya or palm oil is akin to feeding your children chips every day. It is unhealthy and unsustainable. Our Elders know that in pursuing money at all costs, we are going up the creek without a paddle! We are creating a dead end for our species with no way out.

That dead end could be climate chaos, ocean acidification, deforestation, population explosion, famine, drought – a myriad converging crises that could tip humanity towards resource wars and eternal conflict. The question is, why are we racing towards the precipice like a bunch of lemmings when all the evidence shows that our unsustainable lifestyle in search of ever more 'prosperity' does not make us happy? Many philosophers have pondered this question: even in the time of Jesus it is purported that the Apostle Paul said "the love of money is the root of all evil." 2000 years hence and we have still not learned this lesson. Even after the catastrophic financial collapses of the early 21st century and the exposure of the corruption endemic in financial institutions on an epic scale, our governments still extol the virtues of economic growth whilst the gap between richer and poorer grows ever-wider.

Our government's solution to financial ruin is to buy more stuff, build more houses that none of us can afford and produce more consumer goods that have a detrimental effect on ecosystems. Our leaders have lost their vision because they have bought into an economic system that humans invented, that is no longer fit for purpose, yet they tell us there is no alternative!

Mass consumerism has a detrimental effect on ecosystems. © Sculpies ▼

Luckily there is an alternative. In the words of Arundhati Roy the great Indian philosopher and writer, "another world is possible and on a quiet day, I can hear her breathing". I wholeheartedly agree that another world is possible and that there are hundreds of thousands of people all over the world who are facilitating its coming into being. From local currencies to solar farms; from the Transition Network to community-supported agriculture; from the Occupy movements to land redistribution in India; from Youth parliaments to Elders gatherings – another world is happening and we can all be part of it. We do not have to buy into an economic system that will be the perpetrator of our ultimate ruin. We do not have to go down a dead end. In my own small way, by producing and creating eco-fitted furniture that is beautiful, durable and sustainable, I am throwing my lot in with the 'cultural creatives' who know that a better world is possible and that it is happening now.

Another world is possible and on a quiet day, I can hear her breathing.
Arundhati Roy

The complex issues surrounding sustainability are not always evident. Similarly, it's not always clear when we are on a dead end path: when the internal combustion engine was invented it was heralded as the era of personal freedom. Little did we realise that a few decades later, we would be stuck in endless traffic jams, polluting the atmosphere using finite fossil fuels and creating veritable mountains of waste when the vehicles are junked. But we can always make a U-turn. Now, according to EU regulations, 85% of a car by weight has to be recycled or reused and the target is 95% by 2015 – that is amazingly positive progress!

Car designers are now experimenting with a variety of fuels including hybrid-electric and hydrogen, although controversial biofuels seem to be a dead end in their own right. The lessons to be learned from vehicle manufacture are that it is always possible to paddle back down the dead end creek! We are slowly heading in the right direction – there are lots of people working hard to keep the momentum going, and governments must legislate to make it easier for these people by encouraging and supporting the manufacture of products and services that are sustainable. So, whilst a lot of products currently reach a dead end, they don't have to. Most things are potentially recyclable, it just takes time and money and ingenuity as to what used materials could be recycled into. Not everything can be reused or recycled back into itself (like glass, for instance) but can be made into something new – there is a use for everything. Even concrete from derelict buildings can be ground-up and reused as foundations or hardcore for road building and driveways.

Here are some nice example of products that can be made from either recycled or remanufactured materials, such as these beautiful belts made from bicycle tires – I absolutely love them and have two of them.

Shopping trolley upcycled into chic chair, by Max McMurdo ▲

◄ *Modern-day 'rag-and-bone man' Paul Firbank is a designer-maker of furniture and lighting who has an admiration for things that were built to last, which is why he reincorporates scraps of industrial history and end of life vehicles and machines into his new work.*

I am hopeful about the future, but our media is fixated on bad news and negativity. Who chooses the news? Who decides that it is more important to hear about another factory closure than a new recycling centre? The editors and producers of our news programmes have been inculcated that good news isn't interesting and that only bad news sells. We should take heed of the words of former BBC news presenter, Martyn Lewis who issued a renewed call recently for more good news to be reported in the UK media and that constantly reporting bad news is unbalanced, lazy journalism that gives a distorted picture of what the world is really like. "We need the media to engage in solutions-driven journalism where incredibly interesting news comes from" said Lewis.

◄ *Belt made from used bicycle tyres by velo-re*

I believe humans are inherently good, we just don't realise what bad we may be doing, partly because we are misinformed by a media that sees the world through corporate eyes – ones that are only interested in money – and partly because, for myriad reasons, we are not told the whole truth. Take the Inventions Secrecy Act again. We are told there's no credible alternative to fossil fuels because the alternatives have been quashed by vested interests who want to keep the status quo – and their own power – in tact.

What we actually want and need as human beings is a comfortable, peaceful life for all, with the best care for our families and others and with security of food, water and shelter. This is achievable, so we mustn't believe the media that tells us otherwise. As the scandals at NewsCorp have shown, the media has hidden agendas: it is in cahoots with governments and corporations to keep us scared of everything, because if we are scared we spend a lot of money on protection, insurance, saving and amassing money just in case it all goes wrong and for that day when it will all be okay, when we will be free, retired and able to live. I believe it doesn't need to be like that: you need to live your life now and smell the roses along the way!

Upcycled ring-pull cushions made in Brazil by Da Lata ▲

If we do nothing and carry on as we are we will head towards the dead end I have talked about. Imagine if we keep filling up holes in the ground with poisonous rubbish, eventually we will run out of space for these holes. Endlessly burning fossil fuels in cars, boats, planes and power stations will just choke up the atmosphere. As the world population booms and the developing world moves towards the same levels of consumption as the West, we will run out of resources and conflict will arise. If we keep putting radioactive waste in the ground we leave a toxic legacy for generations to come. If we keep emptying dangerous chemicals into the water then all the fish will die. If we carry on cutting down and burning the rainforest at the current rate of an area the size of one football pitch per second, we will irreversibly alter the climate – and the same goes for every other bad habit we have. And I do believe that this behaviour is just habitual – we are addicted to these lifestyles, but like any addict, we can wean ourselves off them and embrace a cleaner, healthier future.

"When one tugs at a single thing in nature, we find it attached to the rest of the world."
John Muir

Labels: the potential to influence good design

If we knew the truth about where our products come from and how they create a dead end economy, many of us would change our purchasing behaviour. Many people make a point of knowing where the goods they buy come from and labelling has now started to make that process easier. But on the whole, many of us don't know, or worse, don't care about these things, or at least, we don't fully connect with the story behind the product. We may be aware that the term 'ethical clothing' means something positive about the garment, but mostly, we don't appreciate the full story of where and how the clothes are made, and that's a shame, because often these stories can be inspiring. What's on the label can really help consumers to make an informed choice – a vote for a more just and sustainable future and a rejection of the dead end economy.

Manufacturers will go to great lengths to paint their products as whiter than white, when in fact quite the opposite is true. Literally, just look at washing powders: they have beautiful names like Spring Blossom or Jasmine Fresh, yet are produced using chemicals that can and do have a detrimental effect on the environment. They are about as far from a fresh spring morning with the perfume of jasmine on the air as it is possible to get. But, there are always alternatives and these are what I urge you to seek out. When making a purchase, always ask yourself, "do I know how this is made? Do I know the provenance of the raw materials? Do I know who owns the company?" If not, then maybe a bit of online research is in order to satisfy yourself that the whiter than white bed linen you are purchasing doesn't in fact poison the farmers who grow the cotton.

A keen eye on labelling is essential when buying clothes or cars; fridges or skin care products. Labelling can be very confusing: take skin care and cosmetics as an example. Many of them use the term 'organic' but this doesn't mean the ingredients have been produced to the strict organic standards (usually determined by a registered organic symbol) - it simply means that the product contains plant matter, which is literally organic – a naturally-occurring compound – in nature: it's a rather insidious marketing ploy. We know organic is good but we are not too sure why.

Reading the label may not tell you what you need to know. © Mjth ▶

Most labelling does not tell you what's in a product - if it did, no one would buy anything! A label does not say, "this product was made using child labour in a factory with no fire-escapes, and pays the workers less than minimum wage". No! The label will say, "Made in India. 100% cotton. Climate-friendly: can be washed at 30°C." That may be true enough, but it is not the whole story and it is not enough to allow us to make informed decisions. This kind of labelling is designed to confuse us and keep us away from the whole truth. The label deliberately disconnects us from the original source of the raw materials and production processes.

But things are gradually changing for the better. The company Innnocent Smoothie for example, makes a virtue of their labelling. They are proud to tell you about their products: "No Sugar. No Concentrates. No Funny Business". Their labelling makes a joke of the stiff, confusing labelling normally seen on products where minimal information is given and then only to tick regulation boxes. I used Innocent because it is a pretty good example of honest labelling – not perfect mind you – but when I first picked up their product a few years ago and read the whole label, I felt a great deal of satisfaction that change was coming: at last, the beginning of labelling designed for humans to read and understand! I felt this was a product made by people that really care - not just about their product, or making money, but about how their product impacts on people and planet. That is the feeling we should get from everything we buy.

Furniture for the Future by Tristan Titeux

Imagine if you went to the shop and you bought a nice new dress and on the label it said something like this:

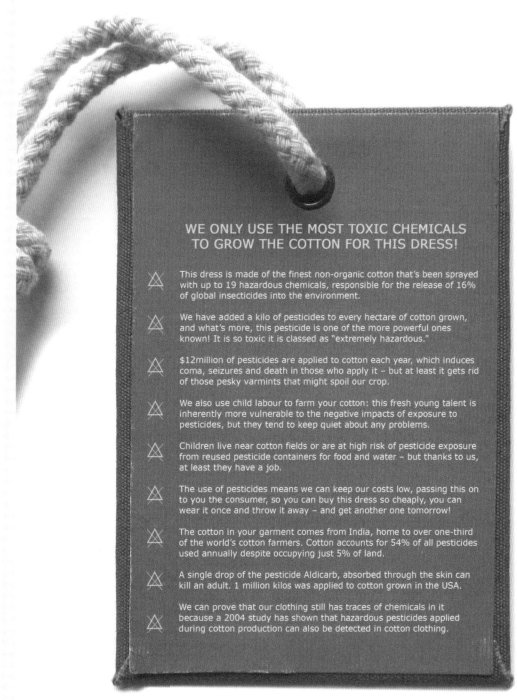

WE ONLY USE THE MOST TOXIC CHEMICALS TO GROW THE COTTON FOR THIS DRESS!

This dress is made of the finest non-organic cotton that's been sprayed with up to 19 hazardous chemicals, responsible for the release of 16% of global insecticides into the environment.

We have added a kilo of pesticides to every hectare of cotton grown, and what's more, this pesticide is one of the more powerful ones known! It is so toxic it is classed as "extremely hazardous."

$12million of pesticides are applied to cotton each year, which induces coma, seizures and death in those who apply it – but at least it gets rid of those pesky varmints that might spoil our crop.

We also use child labour to farm your cotton: this fresh young talent is inherently more vulnerable to the negative impacts of exposure to pesticides, but they tend to keep quiet about any problems.

Children live near cotton fields or are at high risk of pesticide exposure from reused pesticide containers for food and water – but thanks to us, at least they have a job.

The use of pesticides means we can keep our costs low, passing this on to you the consumer, so you can buy this dress so cheaply, you can wear it once and throw it away – and get another one tomorrow!

The cotton in your garment comes from India, home to over one-third of the world's cotton farmers. Cotton accounts for 54% of all pesticides used annually despite occupying just 5% of land.

A single drop of the pesticide Aldicarb, absorbed through the skin can kill an adult. 1 million kilos was applied to cotton grown in the USA.

We can prove that our clothing still has traces of chemicals in it because a 2004 study has shown that hazardous pesticides applied during cotton production can also be detected in cotton clothing.

Who would buy a product if the label was as truthful as that?

People don't want others to suffer on their behalf: we are caring creatures. That is why it is such good news that the production of organic cotton has increased five-fold over the 4 years leading to 2007 – because organic farming methods do not use toxic chemicals, pesticides or fertilisers. They are much more in-tune with nature and do far less damage to the environments where they are grown, and to the farmers who grow them. It is time companies told the entire truth about what they do. Top fashion designer Katherine Hamnett says, "by insisting on organic cotton and fair pay for garment workers, and by paying 1% more for a T-shirt, you can change the world and make it a better, safer place."

Now, imagine that next to the dress you were thinking of buying, there was another rather more expensive one, but with the following label:

I know which one I would buy – and being a man, I don't wear dresses!

- THE DRESS IS MADE OF ORGANIC COTTON THAT WAS GROWN USING NATURAL TECHNIQUES THAT DO NOT HARM THE LOCAL ECOLOGY OF THE FIELDS NOR THE PEOPLE WHO WORK AND PICK THE COTTON

- BECAUSE THE COTTON IS GROWN IN AN ORGANIC SYSTEM WITH OTHER CROPS SUCH AS FRUIT AND NUTS, IT CREATES A DYNAMIC ECOSYSTEM OF BENEFICIAL PLANTS THAT ATTRACT INSECTS WHICH NATURALLY EAT OTHER PESTS – MEANING THERE IS NO NEED FOR PESTICIDE CHEMICALS.

- THESE FRUIT AND NUTS ARE ALSO HARVESTED AFTER THE COTTON, ENSURING A CONSTANT INCOME-STREAM FOR THE SMALL FARMERS WHO TAKE GREAT CARE OF THEIR LAND AND UNDERSTAND THAT IT IS IMPORTANT TO LOOK AFTER IT FOR GENERATIONS TO COME.

- THE FARMER IS PART OF A COOPERATIVE THAT PAYS HIM AND HIS CO-WORKERS VERY WELL FOR THE COTTON CROP. THEY ARE VERY HAPPY AND FEEL GREAT REWARD AND SATISFACTION FOR ALL THE HARD WORK THAT GOES INTO GROWING THE COTTON.

- THE COOPERATIVE THEN PROCESSES THE COTTON USING NATURAL PRODUCTS TO KEEP THE COTTON UNBLEACHED AND HARMLESS TO YOUR SKIN.

- THE COOPERATIVE WEAVES THE FIBRES INTO HIGH-QUALITY CLOTH THAT IS THEN TRANSPORTED BY TRAIN TO THE UK WHERE IT IS MADE INTO YOUR DRESS, IN A FACTORY THAT USES RENEWABLE ELECTRICITY TO RUN ITS MAHINES.

- YOUR DRESS IS PACKED IN A NATURAL HEMP BAG WHICH YOU CAN REUSE AND RECYCLE.

1.2.38

In these days of smartphone technology, all this information could be printed on a barcode and swiped by the consumer, so they can check on the provenance of the goods. But quite rightly, we cannot assume that everyone has access to, or can afford such technology, so some companies are making a virtue of their labels, printing them beautifully on natural papers and making the label something the purchaser would like to keep as a momento. This type of information connects you to the source of the product and gives it a whole lot more meaning. You know the dress is much more healthy for you to wear as you are not breathing chemicals from it that are off-gassing – but you also know that it hasn't asphyxiated anyone else in it's production either. You feel that you have contributed to something special, that you have made a big difference in the world by making your ethical and thoughtful purchase – and that is worth so much more than money! You become part of a community of world citizens who care about each other and the planet.

It makes sense, and more sense is what we need in this confusing world! We don't want to be told lies, or not told the whole truth. If something is so bad it has to be hidden from show, then it should not be done in the first place and is definitely part of the dead end economy. The world is only in the mess that it is because we are dishonest with ourselves and with each other. We can aspire to be the best we can be: the kindest, most honest and most generous.

That is the philosophy which runs through my company Custom Carpentry. I would not sleep properly if I knew I hadn't told you about something that may adversely affect you. I want only the best for you: I want you to be delighted with my product; I want it to exceed your expectations; if I do something you are not happy with I feel like I have failed, so I want to make it perfect and that is what drives me forward. I want to leave a trail of happiness, and contentment! Life is short and I want to have a clear conscience that I have done my best, helped those who needed my help and made a difference to you.

◀ *A QR code allows businesses to tell the whole story behind their product, to make special offers and give information about their business. Try scanning this in on your smart phone to find out about Tristan Titeux, the author of this book.*

We are taught as children to tell the truth and to be honest and that should not change as we become adults. We still need to tell the truth whether we own a small company or are the CEO of a huge multinational that answers to its shareholders. More importantly, the government should tell us the truth, the whole truth and nothing but the truth – but sadly, this is not always the case.

A Fishy Business – how the dead end economy is devastating our oceans

A school of big-eye travelly. © Abdulla Swad ▼

The need for truth in the fishing industry has never been greater. The current methods of fishing with great big nets dredging up everything in their paths, is not sustainable at all. Interestingly, the need for sustainability in the fishing industry is not a new issue. Back in 1376 a petition was presented to Parliament because of a new type of net that had been introduced to trawl the sea. It was described as being "of so small a mesh, no manner of fish, however small, entering within it can pass out and is compelled to remain therein and be taken…by means of which instrument the fishermen aforesaid take so great abundance of small fish aforesaid, that they know not what to do with them, but feed and fatten the pigs with them, to the great damage of the whole commons of the kingdom, and the destruction of the fisheries in like places, for which they pray remedy". Even in 1376, there was an awareness of what over-extraction of one ecosystem can do to the whole.

"It is a curious situation that the sea, from which life first arose, should now be threatened by the activities of one form of that life."
Rachel Carson (*Silent Spring*, 1962)

According to zoologist Les Watling of the University of Hawaii, "bottom trawling is the most destructive of any actions that humans conduct in the ocean". There is currently a fleet of supertrawlers dredging all life from the oceans in nets so vast they could hold 13 jumbo jets – fortunately, many governments have seen fit to ban them, but they are still active in many international waters, and are threatening to trawl that most precious of ecosystems, the Great Barrier Reef, although at the time of writing, the Australian government has seen fit to ban the supertrawlers from their waters for two years.

Another side-effect of this catch-all trawling is that it disturbs the ocean-floor sediment which is where the most resistant chemicals and pollutants come to rest. This then mixes with the plankton ecology that in turn moves back up the food chain into the fish that end up in our bellies. In addition to this, a huge percentage of the catch is thrown back into the ocean, because up to 70% of species caught are regarded as waste, a 'by-catch' that is thrown back into the sea: thousands of fish, dead. This is a bit like buying all the clothes in a shop and then dumping most of them in the bin on the way home. Hardly an efficient process!

Furniture for the Future by Tristan Titeux

If you saw this label on your tin of tuna, would you buy it?

Contains only
the Rarest Tuna

Full of Delicious
Dolphins

GREEDY FLEET

NEARLYGONE TUNA

Ingredients: Contains only the rarest tuna caught from the last 2% of total tuna stocks left in the world. This tuna was caught in giant nets that dredge the bottom of the ocean bed and kills all the sea-life it catches. Over 10 tons or 70% of this 'by-catch' including dolphins, turtles, and sharks is thrown back dead, to leave you with only the tastiest tuna.

Sometimes, when we are bombarded by media stories of doom and gloom, it just seems like people don't really care about each other, but mostly these people are misled: by their governments, and by the media. They would care if they really knew what was going on. Others care but just think they can't do anything about it so carry on with their lives. That may be you? I know you care – that is why you picked up this book: you are interested in learning more, discovering more… You are curious, you like learning about the wider world, you are caring, generous, thoughtful. You like good design and beautiful objects that take time and care to create. You are a person who can change the world: you can make such a difference just by the things you buy! Money is power and it is currently the universal language of our civilisation – and until we invent better ways of doing things, it is your only true democratic voting system! If you don't like something, don't buy into it.

We live as part of the wider world community, not in an isolated country where we can shove our problems under the carpet and forget about them. We need to take responsibility, and the only people to do that are us – the people. Governments are an important part of the whole thing, in fact a vital part, but governments are influenced by you – and companies – but those companies are run by you and influenced by those who shop with them, so although it is comforting to think that we can sit and wait for the government sort this all out, it won't happen. You, the consumer, are in charge.

Believe in yourself, believe that you are powerful, and that change happens because you make it happen, not someone else.

1.3

WHY CARE FOR THE ENVIRONMENT?

"Our modern, industrial economy takes a mountain covered with trees, lakes, running streams and transforms it into a mountain of junk, garbage, slime pits and debris."
Edward Abbey

We should care for the environment because it isn't ours to destroy. We take care of our children, we owe it to them, so it is imperative we leave them a liveable planet too. Most of us wouldn't throw our rubbish around when walking in the countryside or in a beautiful park – so why as a society do we throw our rubbish away in a great big hole in the ground, which we call landfill? According to David Wann (*Buzzworm* 1990) "The packaging for a 'microwave dinner' is programmed for a shelf life of maybe six months, a cook time of two minutes and a landfill dead-time of centuries".

If you zoom out of the earth via Google Earth or similar, you will see that nature is our big park. Sadly, it is dotted with litter, holes full of rubbish, and dumps everywhere. We must look further than our immediate surroundings, and understand that we will not be the last ones to live on this beautiful planet. Our children would like to have a clean future too.

People argue about climate change and other environmental issues: is it really happening? is organic any better for you? is it too late…? How can some people try to tell us that the world is not warming abnormally when almost 50% of the ice shelf melted in the summer of 2012? What is their agenda? How can anyone say organic is not good for you – if it is good for the animals and for the environment, which it undoubtedly is, then it is good for you.

Let these people argue amongst themselves. Meanwhile, follow your own intuition – what is true and real for you? Talk to those who understand or who are open to new possibilities. It is a fact of life that people have vastly differing opinions: that is part of nature's diversity plan. The bad is there to show us that if we go too far we will get in trouble, and the good is there to moderate the bad. A perfect balance is rarely achieved by humanity – but is often the state of pristine nature. It is within our own nature to live in balance and harmony. We simply have to cultivate the inner knowledge and wisdom to recognise it.

Our internal dialogue will comfort us by saying "it's not that bad," "I'm OK," "it could be worse," "I'm still alive," "it never did me any harm." With these comforting words we justify certain life situations, but at the root of them it is obvious that we aren't living in a state of balance. If we were, we would say, "I am happy," "all is well," "I am fulfilled," etc. This applies to everything we do in life: our relationships, businesses... everything. Our inner talk is there to make us feel better about what we are doing. That is how people can do very bad things, yet persuade themselves that it is totally normal and they are doing no harm. The key is to cultivate the wisdom to tell the difference between self-deception and reality.

▲ *Extraction of bauxite in the middle of the Amazon.* © *iStockphoto*

If you watch and read about gruesome things, this eventually normalises them. People become inured to violence. They think what they are doing is OK, whether it is making consumer decisions that impact on the planet or whether they mistreat their animals. People don't realise what harm they are really doing, because society teaches us not to care.

We all do the same: we have behavioural tendencies that do us harm. What do you say to yourself when you want a big, sweet, tasty, chocolate, calorie-ridden dessert? "It's okay," "it's only once," "I deserve it," "I have worked hard," or "it's the weekend," (every weekend!). We justify damaging behaviour to normalise it. Okay, it's maybe not the best example. It's fine to treat yourself – in fact, it is necessary to do so. But if you did that every night and made excuses to yourself, then eventually, you'd become ill.

We should take care of the environment now, because what we do to the Earth, we do to ourselves. If we constantly flush bleach, medication and detergents down the drains, in the end, we are flushing them down our own throats. Everything in nature cycles and recycles, so it bears repeating – what we do to the Earth, we do to ourselves. We need to trust ourselves more and listen to our natural instincts. Since when did it make sense to destroy the rainforest? Imagine if we do carry on burning and clearing the rainforest. What will that mean for carbon sequestration and the state of the atmosphere – because ultimately, the rainforests are the lungs of the planet and without them, we cannot breathe?

Many places in the world don't have the ability to cleanse their water supply like we do, but even our best efforts at cleaning water are not good enough. I don't take any chances, and have a reverse osmosis filter, which comprises no less than 5 different filters that are supposed to clean it 100%. But where do all the chemicals that are filtered out go?

Drugs, steroids, pharmaceuticals, cosmetics, shampoos, soaps and the contraceptive pill all end up in the effluent from sewage treatment plants, then into waterways. They make it into our bodies from drinking water, and into the bodies of fish. A third of male fish in British rivers are in the process of changing sex due to pollution by human sewage. Research by the Environment Agency survey found that of 1500 fish at 50 river sites, more than a third of males displayed female characteristics. Imagine what this is doing to us, who eat the fish!

Poorly designed packaging ends up polluting rivers, seas and landfill. ▼

It could be considered that this is nature's way of balancing its system: by getting rid of a few humans who are the source of the problem! But human beings are ingenuous creatures – we can easily devise systems that don't create our own demise.

Nature will always be one-step ahead of human beings, because ultimately, we are part of nature, not apart from nature: as soon as we realise that we can't control nature but must live in harmony with natural systems, then so much the better. Even though this may mean using the height of our technological ingenuity, we will all be the richer, including our planetary systems. We must live by nature's rules.

Humanity has always influenced nature, of course – just like a child will often say words of wisdom to a parent, but for every influence we put nature's way there is a consequence, just like a vacuum or a see-saw. If you put more of an influence in one direction, you may unbalance something in the other: a vacuum is created that needs to be filled with something else. You can't just shift something from one place to another and think that you have got rid of the problem: that is ignorance.

There is a consequence for every action we take.

For every action there is also an equal and opposite reaction. For every yin there is a yang. So what we do to the Earth we must do thoughtfully and with an awareness that it will have consequences elsewhere: but can we limit the consequences or do things differently? My aim in this book, as in life, is to concentrate on solutions and making things better, so I choose to focus on the positive side, aiming to promote as much positivity in the world as possible: I want to create more yin, to balance the considerable yang that seems to dominate our lives. It helps to remember that each of us is a tiny part of a much greater organism. We are like ants in a colony, microbes in a body, tiny cells in the infinite universe. We are part of a greater whole, and we work together like an organism.

Furniture for the Future by Tristan Titeux

With this in mind, obviously it doesn't make any sense to eat cancerous chemicals that are sprayed on crops and pumped into meat – or into our furnishings, and everything we own. So why do we allow this psychopathic corporate behaviour? To some degree it is because we want everything for nothing. We don't care about how it affects others, or even about how it affects us, as long as it is cheap. Our drive towards cheap goods at any cost (even the ultimate cost of the health of the planet) is pushing us, lemming-like, towards an ecological precipice and it seems there is little we can now do to stop it.

If we breathe a vehicle away that products are same levels of toxins currently emitted by vehicles, it would never get a patent. © Diego Vito Cervo ▶

"Give a man a fish and he can eat for a day, but teach a man how to fish and he'll be dead of mercury poisoning inside of three years."
Charles Haas

What will happen if we ignore the warning signs nature is currently expressing, and carry on with business-as-usual? Well, scientists tell us that we've reached the tipping-point, beyond which there is no return to a balanced and harmonious natural world. It is in our interests to do all we can today to redress the balance and help heal the wounds we have inflicted on nature.

Just project yourself into the future, say in 200 years. What will our great-great grandchildren think of us? They will look back at us now, like we look back at the Middle Ages, and ask: "what on earth happened? These people were intelligent: they went to the moon and they created the most amazing things like planes and computers. And yet they were filthy in their behaviour: they dumped sewage and chemicals in the sea, dumped poisonous rubbish on the earth, cut down all the trees, and came close to cutting the life cord from themselves. How lucky we are to have made it through and be alive today! But what a mess we have been left with!"

Our children have the right to a clean environment like that which our parents knew. We owe it to our children to take care of the environment for them. We have not been given it to abuse until every last resource is used up in the shortest period of time. We have been loaned it by our children – we are looking after it for them.

We are now in a great position: we can make a big difference very quickly and reach a wide range of people. We live in the digital age, where information travels fast. Thanks to social media, we can get messages of any sort out as far and fast as possible. We are now entering a revolution, the like of which has not been seen before. Now, we do not need to rely on the corrupted and corporatised mainstream media that has, for so long, told us what to do. Now, we can learn the truth about what is really happening on the beautiful planet directly from the people who it is happening to. We *can* project our opinion and make ourselves heard, and through amazing social networks like Avaaz and 38 Degrees, we *can* do something about what we feel is psychopathic behaviour towards the earth. It's time to care for the environment now – before it is too late.

1.4

WHAT'S IN IT FOR YOU?

Fairtrade – good choices for good causes

When you help someone, you feel good – you get a great sense of satisfaction. So why not make a choice that extends that understanding? If you know that you have made an ethical choice and bought a product that is made with care, that does not exploit people or the environment, then you will see added value in that purchase. If you fully understand the implications of your actions then you will feel great satisfaction. If you have a painting, you know it is beautiful, but if you know about the artist, their life story and beliefs, that makes the painting become a work of art, special to you because you connect with it in more than just a visual way. If you meet someone else who likes this art you feel a connection. This analogy can be extended to all aspects of life and is epitomised in ethical consumerism, most recently, the Fairtrade Movement

What does it say about the way the world is run, if we need goods that are labelled Fairtrade? Surely all trade should be fair?

The closer you are to the source of a product or service, the more connected you feel and the more satisfaction you get from your purchase. Support your local farmers' market if you can or buy from an organic vegetable and food delivery scheme, which will support British farmers. Look for fairly traded imported fruit such as the bananas that we love, but can't grow here.

Many farmers are exploited by supermarkets that dictate prices to such an extent, farmers make little or no profit – that is why cutting out the middle man and buying directly from farmers' markets is such a help to the ailing industry. Currently, two farmers per day in the UK sell up. Should Fairtrade relate just to imports? I think not. I think we should look at what is going on in our country too. We are taught at school and by our parents to be fair, kind and generous to others. When we grow up, does that all go out the window? Or is it just that we don't know the facts: if we had cocoa plantations in the UK and saw children of 12 years working hard for 50p per day there would be an outcry.

Organic foods contain no petrochemicals, no harmful pesticides and the animals have lived a happy life outdoors, eating grass, running around, sun-bathing, dust-bathing, mingling with each other, eating good organic feed – not being injected with growth promoters and antibiotics that are then passed on to humans. Everything is connected and we are what we eat! The healthier food our animals eat, the fresher the grass and the slower-maturing the breed, the more exercise they get, and the happier their state of mind, the tastier the meat. Indeed, we too need to slow down, eat less, live slower lives, and appreciate what we have. Fast, fast, fast does no good – not to our bodies or to the food we eat. The Slow Food movement is a testament to this fact.

Connectivity:
you're part of the web of life

Dew drops on a spider's web © Diane Picard ▶

There is great satisfaction in knowing that through your consumer choices you are helping towards maintaining something much bigger than just you and your life. You don't feel so alone because you feel like you can make a difference in the world. You may be a tiny part of a massive universe, but you are just as important as any other being because you are connected to it all – directly and indirectly you are part of a web, a huge web, and if you pull on the web in one place it will be felt in other places to varying degrees.

Knowing the story behind your furniture, home furnishings and other belongings, will, I hope, increase the enjoyment you get out of them. You will look at things in a new way and ask more questions than you did before. You will wonder how things are made, who made them, how long it took, what materials were used, where they came from. In nature you may think more deeply about a beautiful tree and how long it may have stood, what it may have seen and what it has yet to see. If a tree could speak it would teach us so much: it is a silent witness to so much history.

Have you ever been on an outing and not really been into the journey? Maybe a school trip, or if abroad, maybe you went on a tour and were not that interested in the destination. If so you probably didn't connect well, didn't understand and found it boring – but imagine the opposite: you know about the place you are visiting, you are interested in finding out more and you have an amazing guide who is passionate about it and is telling you more. You feel like you are in another world, you really connect and enjoy the experience. Even though the place may be just ruins and rocks, the closer you are to the source and the more you know, the more you enjoy and respect it.

Likewise, when you care about the purchase choices you make, you will appreciate the history behind the item more: you will be interested in what it is made of, who made it, how and why. You will see yourself as part of its story and you will feel the connectivity. You won't look at anything in a two dimensional way anymore, instead when you look at something you will get a warm glow from the understanding of the history behind it, and what makes it the way it is.

Through this book and my work, I hope to show how to make a big difference with everyday choices; it doesn't mean that you need to start wearing sandals and sackcloth and eat salad and rice! That isn't the way of the world, that isn't the way we have evolved, we are modern human beings with a modern life and that is okay. But we do need to be more aware of how we affect our environment. We need to become more curious and not accept everything without question. I believe cars are fine, we need cars, but we need good cars that we can recycle and reuse: it is now possible to create renewable, non-polluting vehicles, so it makes sense to choose them. You can make a difference, and that is exciting and empowering.

> "The creation of a thousand forests is in one acorn."
> Ralph Waldo Emerson

People creating change

Don't think for a minute that it is all up to you. There are people who spend all their time campaigning for change. It is a tireless process that requires total dedication to the cause and that is why the government eventually does make changes. These people need our support. For example, the FSC (Forest Stewardship Council) was established in 1993 thanks to the efforts of campaigners and Fairtrade organisations. The FSC is a non-profit company, devoted to encouraging the responsible management of the world's forests. The FSC sets high standards that ensure forestry is practised in an environmentally responsible, socially beneficial and economically viable way. FSC principles are strict and closely monitored: they ensure that natural forests are conserved, that endangered species and their habitats are protected, and that forest workers and forest dependent communities are respected. The FSC also has a rigorous chain of custody, tracing timber from the forest to the end use. The FSC enjoys support from conservation groups, indigenous communities and forest product buyers. The FSC gives equal decision-making rights to economic, social and environmental interests in its governing structure and standard setting process.

So, if you want to support healthy forests and communities, ask for the FSC label when purchasing wood or paper products. It is people who are passionate about change that get things moving and you can help – we can all help create change for the better in our millions and billions by choosing to spend our money in the right places and on the right things.

Acorn germination. © Danijel Micka ▲

> "The trees that are slow to grow, bear the best fruit."
> Moliere (1622 – 1673)

◄ *The English oak is an icon of the British countryside.*

When making a purchase ask "how will this purchase impact on my world? Do I want to make a difference with this money?" Money makes the world go around and is the most powerful way we currently have to vote about the ethics of corporate systems. We are spending money all the time so we are voting all the time: we are not waiting for an election every four years to cast our vote, we are always voting! That is real democracy: the power to choose which systems of production we want to support. Do we want systems that enslave young children or do we want to support systems that pay farmers well for their work? It really is as simple as that. Of course, we need money to be able to vote this way, but we don't necessarily need money to help the environment. Many campaigners have little money, but instead use time and ingenuity.

Furniture for the Future by Tristan Titeux

> "Switch to organic produce and to green electricity today, and you will instantly make a world of difference."

Given a simple matter of choice, when money is taken out of the equation, most people will make the right choices. If you said to someone "do you choose that which is unhealthy for you, that pollutes the environment and enslaves others to produce, or do you choose the organic, healthy option that doesn't pollute and tastes much better?" then it seems that the answer should be obvious, but if you don't understand what you are choosing and why one is better than the other, then it is likely that you will be led by price and naturally you will want to save your money. Isn't it amazing how we are so used to money ruling our lives? Most of us lead lives dictated by money: where we live, where we shop, where we go. Most of our choices are decided by the money we have in our pockets. Remove the money factor and just imagine what the world would look like! Seriously, I am making the point that we let money rule our lives and guide our choices too often. We use money as an excuse for not making good choices.

We are dragging all life out of the sea because it makes money for someone. We make cocaine and pour chemicals into the Amazon because it makes money for someone. We use growth-hormones on animals and rear fast-growing breeds that can't stand up because they are too heavy, and feed them cheap food because it makes money for someone. More money, made faster and faster until everything implodes. As a society, we cannot continue to allow money to rule the world like it does, because it makes no sense to pollute our planet simply to make money. We need to exercise more common sense, more empathy, more care and respect for our natural world.

Money is ambiguous: it does not distinguish between good and evil, yet it is the main currency we use. Love and generosity, compassion, peace and respect should be our primary currency. Money should serve to facilitate the exchange of ethical goods that respect the primary currency.

> "Know those things that lead to your wellbeing, and those things that lead to your destruction."
> American Indian traditional code of ethics

Is the madness of the stock exchange the best way to make decisions about our future? Billions of dollars change hands every day, with no thought for the impact this has on the environment. We are all connected and the decisions taken here affect all of us. © AmericanSpirit ▶

Food and health

Choosing to have fitted furniture (or any other product for that matter) that is earth friendly will open you up to all sorts of other changes: knowing why your furniture is eco-friendly will help you appreciate what it has taken for it to exist. This paradigm will lead you to look at your health and your food and you will start to question this too. You will have learned more about the origin of things and will understand that your possessions and your health are more connected than you thought. Once you understand why eco-materials make sense, you will apply the same thinking in your whole way of life. You will enjoy your food more and start to make healthier choices leading to a positive new path that is non-destructive and beneficial to your health and to the natural world around you.

I live to eat! Food has taught me most of what I know about the environment: because I have always been interested in food it has led me to learn where it all comes from and how it is produced. It has taught me to be curious and to find more ethical sources for my food and get really involved in these choices. I have to eat three times a day, so I might as well make it as enjoyable and meaningful as I can. In the end, food and shelter are all we need to survive, so let's make decisions about them as thoughtfully as possible.

Most people relate to food, so that is a good place to start. There are not many people who don't like food, although there are those who say things like, "I don't like cheese," or "I don't drink water," or "I don't like tomatoes," etc. There are foods I prefer more than others, but there are few things that I will not eat. Anyway, I relate to food, but it is possible to use the same theories and examples for anything you buy. It really doesn't matter what example is used: it is a pattern that can be superimposed onto other areas of your life, whether it be food, fitted furniture, your home furnishings, clothes, jewellery etc. It is all related.

> The art of medicine consists in amusing the patient while nature cures the disease.
> Voltaire (1694 - 1778)

Every chemical that is supposedly benign, when mixed with others, can create compounds which have properties that can adversely affect health. It is hard enough for scientists to discover the side-effects of individual chemicals we have in our carpets, the fire retardants in our sofas, the chemicals sprayed on our fruit and vegetables or the drugs pumped into our animals, let alone the impacts of a multitude of such chemicals on our health. We inhale, absorb through our skin and ingest so many different chemicals these days that it is almost impossible to judge what effects these have on our health.

Organic carrots. © Voltan I ▶

My friend Emma Holister beautifully illustrates the way that we are constantly being told what is safe within the limits recommended by the World Health Authority. The fact is we have no idea how all these chemicals combine and what the results are on our health. It is uneconomical and impossible to start testing the infinite number of combinations of chemical reactions from all the chemicals we are subjected to in our lives. The research that is done for the chemicals is carried out by the companies themselves and regulated by bodies who are in the pay of these companies. My belief is that what we are told about the supposedly safe amounts of chemicals in everyday products is suspect. It makes no sense to me to put any dangerous chemical in my body or into the environment, no matter how small, and that is why I always chose the natural, organic alternative, where possible.

Illustration by Emma Holister, health campaigner ▶

So why have we not all succumbed to the effects of accumulated poisoning? Because our bodies are amazing and have very complex and sophisticated defence mechanisms that fight against most of the toxins we subject them to. The environment has always had toxic elements in it: the whole of nature contains good, neutral and harmful natural chemicals. Our bodies have evolved to adapt to these and to overcome some of the poisonous effects. Poisons are chemicals that our bodies have not found a way to deal with and therefore they have a harmful effect on us. In the past 100 years or so due to new manufacturing methods we have seen a huge increase of chemicals compounds, which are mostly man-made. We use them in our medicines, in our food, in our clothes and in all the products and furnishings in our homes.

Our bodies have to fight hard to deal with all these chemicals and it wears the body out. We don't have any idea what these chemicals do because it is such a complex process. Our bodies are amazing but we need help to keep them fit and healthy and drinking water that contains chemicals, eating fast food with all sorts of artificial additives, flavourings and preservatives, consuming inorganic produce that contains more of the same, and living with furnishings that contain yet more chemicals means that our bodies are now prone to cancers, allergies and a myriad other illnesses of modern life.

We are lucky to live in the times that we do – I would not turn back time in any way! We live longer than ever due to amazing drugs we now have, we have cleaner hospitals and all sort of healthcare support, but despite a better standard of living we are still getting very ill and new diseases are cropping up all the time. We are able to live with illness for years now and a lot of older people are supported by medication to live longer: but while life expectancy may be better, quality of life isn't always that good.

We don't want to admit to the problems, but how are we really, as a society? Stress is killing us. Cancer, heart disease, diabetes etc. are on the increase. Many people are depressed and unhappy. Most people past the age of 30 begin to think more about their health. They begin to notice little things about their body and feel that their health cannot be taken for granted as it was when they were younger. So, caring for the environment, saving the earth around us, ultimately, means saving ourselves. Not drinking chemicals from our water supply, or ingesting chemicals with our food, breathing clean air both outside and inside, surrounding ourselves by natural materials… all these things will make us healthier.

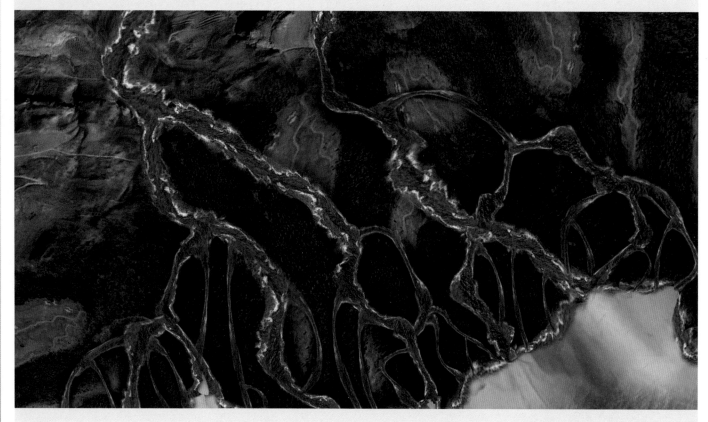

▲ Artist's impression of river tributaries showing striking similarity to blood vessels. © Gil Geolingo

Inside of us is a microcosm of the world outside: inside us is a jungle, a rainforest, a universe that is all related to the outer world (think how much our lungs look like tree roots and branches or the tributaries of a river), so that what we learn about the universe and the natural world we can also apply to our bodies. We rely too much on drugs which should be used as a last resort. We know they work well in an emergency, but a lot of things that nature has to offer work much better and more in harmony with our bodies.

Nature's medicine works with the body to strengthen its immune system and to fight disease: it is not the medicine itself that fights the disease but the body's immune system that is helped by the medicine. I see the body and how it works as akin to a rainforest or any complex undisturbed natural system. The way antibiotics work is a bit like a bomb dropped in enemy territory: it eradicates the enemy successfully but also eradicates the flora and fauna for miles around. Natural medicine I compare to the SAS creeping into the forest, using local knowledge and intelligence to ambush the enemy with no disturbance to the rest of the forest. Natural medicine may take longer to effect a cure and it can be more expensive, but it is a much better solution.

Furniture for the Future by Tristan Titeux

Is it really good for your health?

You can tell if something is good for your health in many ways. Firstly, start with raw materials: whole foods like apples wheat, honey or any vegetables or fruits – how they are processed from that original material into an end product makes a difference as to how healthy it ends up.

We are so far removed from the original source that is it hard to see where things have come from. To really understand things we have to go back to bare bones, to 'expose the roots' without all the fluff that surrounds it. As long as you know the source of any foodstuff, you can work out how good it is for you – and that generally means keeping it natural. To understand this it is useful to know the two extremes so that you can use that for comparison and see at what point on the scale a particular thing you are studying is. For example an ultimate good example of the best thing for you is if you imagine climbing a cherry tree: you see this nice red cherry hanging low and warmed by the sun, you open your mouth and close it around the cherry and pull it off its stalk and chew it slowly and enjoy it's warm, fresh, sweet taste. Well that is the most natural, most unprocessed unadulterated way you could possibly eat a cherry (and if you ever have the chance to go cherry picking go for it!). No processing has occurred from the time you picked the cherry with your mouth and ingested it. That is the standard that you can use for the best.

The closer a foodstuff is to its original state, the better it is for you and the planet, and the more sustainable it is.

Sweet cherries. © Enewa ▶

Then at the other end of the scale there is 'cherry juice' that has been made using chemical flavours made with tens of different artificial chemicals to make a flavouring to taste like cherry. Then it is combined with white sugar which is highly processed, heated, bleached and generally had the living daylights beaten out of it, including any goodness that would have originally been in the sugar such as vitamins, minerals, proteins, enzymes and other beneficial nutrients. In the case of strawberry flavouring, 49 chemical compounds made from petroleum derivatives and others sources are mixed with highly processed natural or artificial flavourings and preservatives.

So, if you go to a shop and see some cherry juice that has natural concentrated cherry juice in it then it is somewhere half way between the two extremes. Organic cherry juice with no sugar and pressed cherries would be the better end and a cherry juice with mostly white refined sugar and cherry flavourings and lots of E-numbers would be the worst case. Of course it helps to have an idea of what cherry concentrate is, what refined sugar means in terms of health and environment etc. Once you know what is in your food or produce then you can better know if you want it or not. That is why honest labelling is crucial. Just like the 'white goods' have A and B ratings, our food labels should have some sort of easy-to-understand labelling systems too – then you would not need a degree in food science to go shopping!

Before you buy something, ask how much processing the product has gone through: the more processing something had, the more likely it is to be bad for your health and the less good it is for the environment. Like in the cherry example, the more you remove something from its natural state, the more energy you need to do so, and in a bad system the more nasty chemicals are needed to produce it. If a product is processed, its molecular structure is changed and tampered with, turning something natural into something potentially dangerous. Nature gives us what we need: a fruit or vegetable is full of life and good things for your body, but once you heat it and cook it you kill-off a lot of these things and the more you cook it, beat it, separate it, mix chemicals with it, stretch it etc., the more you take it further and further away from its original source – and remember the original source is the best.

Ask yourself, is the source derived from petrol, mineral or plants? Plant material, if it hasn't been highly processed, is generally better for you and the environment but can be made toxic with too much manipulation and processing. Petrol by-products are not that great for you as they off-gas chemical vapour, (smell your bin bag next time you open up a new one, and check the smells that come off it).

Humanity's arrogance loves to try to beat nature, but rarely can – nature has taken millions of years to perfect itself! We spend time making a drug to beat nature and nature comes to bite back with a new virus or strain of the disease that is even bigger and stronger than the last. The battle is a never ending one that we cannot win because nature knows all the tricks. If you look at the rainforest, there is a wonderful example of diversity for everything lives together and benefits each other. If we want to be truly healthy, we need to follow this example: take what nature gives us and keep away as much as possible from too highly-processed goods.

A final example of how natural is always best is that of chickens. Originally, they lived in forests and would scratch around on the forest floor for their food. That is the healthiest place for a chicken to exist: outdoors in nature eating grass and bugs. Imagine then, the life of a factory-farmed chicken, crammed in a tiny cage with no straw, grass or daylight. They start to produce bad fats and develop illnesses, so are fed antibiotics because disease can spread fast in such an intensive system. Not great for the chickens of for the humans who consume them. The opposite is of course, the free-range hen who lives outside, eating organic grain, being totally free to run around, maybe in a bit of woodland too. No drugs, lots of grass and bugs to eat – that is the way nature intended life for a chicken. So, I hope I know which system you will choose!

A healthy, happy chicken will give us good, healthy eggs. So therefore, an unhappy, unhealthy chicken will not give us good, healthy eggs.
© S P Flaum

Furniture for the Future by Tristan Titeux

1.5

THE REAL COST

It doesn't cost more to use natural materials!

Products made with conventional materials might seem cheap – but their true cost is not reflected in the financial price at the point of sale. Many costs to people and the environment are not factored in to the equation. Someone else has to pay the price of pollution, of bad working practices and of exploitation (both of people and resources). So that's why products from small ethical companies often seem to cost 'more'. But that's because their workers are paid better, they are not able to use economies of scale and labour-intensive methods, they use less common materials, have a smaller market and work locally, with local costs of living. Ethical products don't cost more: rather, their price is a true reflection of real and fair costs.

> "We're finally going to get the bill for the Industrial Age. If the projections are right, it's going to be a big one: the ecological collapse of the planet."
> Jeremy Rifkin (*World Press Review*, 1989)

Companies operating in large markets have huge economies of scale. What's more, they have many workers in countries where labour is cheap, materials are cheap, and laws are lax. Both the environment's and workers' rights can be easily disregarded. Of course, these producers make cheaper goods compared to many local producers. But the advantage of local producers isn't just a higher quality product. Cheap foreign labour doesn't support your local economy, and it's fundamentally unfair.

It's an illusion that imported goods are cheaper. All this effectively means is that money in some countries is worth less. We can wear cheap clothes in this country because the playing field is not level. If workers in countries like India and China were paid the same as us, then there would be no such thing as cheap clothes! Imported goods would actually be more financially expensive, because you would have to also pay for shipping (and that's leaving aside the environmental costs of shipping or air-freighting).

Who suffers for your cheap goods? The children who are enslaved in garment factories, who can't really be children, because they are working such long hours. They are missing out on an important part of their life and skipping an important part of growing up. Would you send your 13 year old child to work in a factory for 12 hours a day? Some people have no choice about it.

The price of cheap goods is deceptive. Some of the best examples of how 'cheap' is only 'cheap' in monetary terms can be seen in our food. Have you ever seen a chicken for sale, cooked and ready to eat for £3.50? You can't produce a chicken for that price without cutting some serious corners. The chicken needs to be hatched, fed with grain, and looked after. Then it must be killed, plucked, gutted, packaged, sent to market, distributed to shops, cooked and served. How can you possibly do all that for £3.50? It would cost £3.50 just to post that chicken in England – probably more! (Not that you would want to do that...)

A farmer I once met in a farm shop told me a story about a lady who was complaining that his £12 chickens were too expensive. He said to her that she could go to the barn at the back, catch a chicken, kill it, pluck it, gut it and come back and tell him how much she wanted to be paid for doing that! I have killed and processed my own chicken before, just to see if I could. I like to do things myself, but believe me, I don't think I will ever do that again. It is incredibly unpleasant. It stinks when you open it up: you want to be sick. The killing part is not great either, and worst of all is the plucking. It takes forever – so difficult and tedious! I have also brought up baby chicks, feeding and watering them every day. After all that, I think I would sell my chickens for £100! It makes you realise that a £12 chicken is actually really good value. It is much better to eat one good free-range organic chicken once a week for £12, rather than a £4 chicken three times a week, stuffed as it is, full of antibiotics and soya protein imported from Brazil where once a rainforest stood.

Farm shop © Ryan Simpson ▼

We always talk about financial costs – never health, environmental or social costs. The strangest thing about our obsession with financial costs is that other costs, in the end, become financial costs as well. The difference is that someone else pays – and usually, in far distant lands. With certain products such as oil (which is used in everything from T-shirts and medicine to food) the government pays in the form of wars. In other cases governments (that is to say, we) pay with hospital bills due to bad health from eating or absorbing chemicals that induce cancers or heart disease. In the future, our children will also pay to clean up all the pollution left by these man-made chemicals. In effect, we are borrowing money from them to pay for our over-consumption and waste.

Then think about the damage being done to our society. With manufacturing and other jobs going abroad, our children feel they have nothing to do, and many have few job prospects. This is exacerbated by people coming into the country en masse and working for low wages. This pushes out local workers and keeps wages low for everyone else. That leads to more unemployment – something that we all pay a price for. Buying local empowers communities.

But remember, buying natural, local products empowers your local community. It gives local people worthwhile employment so they feel they are valued members of the community. They can see friends and neighbours using their goods or services, and become an integral and appreciated part of their local community.

Let's not blindly consume as if goods simply materialised themselves into existence

There is a very good reason for cheap things being cheap. It's not because someone is doing you a favour. Cheap goods are attractive, but they are not part of a sustainable solution – they are part of the dead-end economy. Either they are poor quality, or someone or something has suffered to create it. I always buy the best I can – something I learned from my father.

My dad never spared a penny on anything and always got us the best. He wasn't rich – we had few things. But the things we had were the best things: good, healthy things. If you can afford it, always go for the best. Not only will it last longer, it will also be more sustainable, more beautiful and give longer-lasting satisfaction than something that is cheap, doesn't work well and doesn't look great.

"Buy cheap and you buy twice." This is what a customer once said to me in a video testimonial – and I couldn't agree more. If you buy a cheap suitcase, the zip breaks. It will cause you stress when it does, and the item will look ugly and cheap – not a very satisfying thing to be pulling around. If you buy some cheap plastic shoes, they just don't feel the same as real leather ones that are nicely designed and built to last. It is obvious really – things are cheap for a reason.

Furniture for the Future by Tristan Titeux

"The so-called choice between going green or going for growth is a false one. Sooner or later, economics and ecology will need to be recognised as two complimentary faces of the same coin."

Tony Juniper

1.6

LEARNING FROM OTHER CIVILISATIONS

Lessons from the 'Elders'

I spend a fair amount of time examining how native – or more accurately, 'First Nations' people live. I like to refer to them as our 'Elders' because they are from a generation of wisdom-keepers who have not forgotten the old, more sustainable, ways. Because they live a 'simpler' life than us, and have been doing so for a very long time, it is relatively easy to get a good idea of what they do – and how and why they do it. I always conclude that what makes a good life can be summed-up fairly easily: we don't need much to live happily. The things that drive most of us forward are basic survival needs – like air, food, water and shelter – as well as fundamental social needs like love, friendship, and work. Everything else is just a distraction.

◄ Familly spending time together © Stefan Lubo www.stefanlubo.com

I am not suggesting we should live like aborigines or native people. Rather, we should compare their philosophies and ways of life to our own modern lives, to see if we are going in the right direction.

Aboriginal society tends to be collectivist, summed-up by the phrase "we all look after one another." Non-Aboriginal culture, on the other hand, is individualist: "look after yourself." The latter approach tends to isolate us and make us feel that we are not part of a greater good. It is important to learn from the Aborigines, and see that if we look after others we will also be looking after ourselves.

We have taken on too much of the philosophy of "looking out for number one." This is a very selfish and destructive attitude. It doesn't encourage us to look at how our actions affect the world around us. Of course we must look after 'number one' – but not to the detriment of everyone and everything else. We are part of something larger than ourselves.

We are lucky to live in such an amazing time. I certainly don't want to turn back time – but I would encourage people to take the best from the past. It makes sense that the people that have been on the planet for a long time, who have lived in harmony with it and understand it, are the best people to ask about how to live on it.

In many of the things we do, we just need to stop and think: have we gone too far with this? We just need to step back a little, to understand what it is we are doing that is out of balance. It means accepting that we have made mistakes, and that we need to get back on track. For example, sometimes mass production just isn't the best way: mass production is great for producing screws, nuts and bolts but not tasty healthy food.

Take only what you need today.

Furniture for the Future by Tristan Titeux

Original native tribes respected their land. Australian Aborigines would travel around looking for food. When they stopped in a place, they would make a fire – and in the morning when they moved on, they would cover it over to leave no trace that they had been there at all.

You could say: "how much of a problem is a little hole with a few stones and ash in the centre going to be if you leave it? Australia is so big – what is the big deal?" It's true that with time, the tribe's presence would be virtually undetectable anyway. But that isn't the point. The Aborigines' practice shows a deep respect for the earth. Once they had disturbed nature, they wanted to put it back to how it was – as if no one had been there. If only our modern culture would take a leaf out of their book.

This is a simple example of how we can learn from the ways of native people. There is nothing to complicate the issue. It's not like modern life with lots of things to consider and interpret. It's just a simple rule: leave things how you would want them to be found.

If you take an issue back to its roots you can understand more easily – it's as simple as eating the cherry straight from the tree. If you have a clear, straightforward example, you can measure other things against it. And even if all we learn from the Aborigines is that we should clean up our mess when we move on, then we will still have learned a lot!

"We are all visitors to this time, this place. We are just passing through. Our purpose here is to observe, to learn, to grow, to love… and then we return home."
Aboriginal philosophy

The Aborigines only took what they needed. They understood that they had to leave something for other species and future generations. They did not strip a tree of all its fruit, leaving it bare – they just took a few fruits and moved on. The principle 'take only what you need today' is a central traditional Aboriginal value. In contrast, non-Aboriginal culture often operates under the capitalist value of 'accumulate for tomorrow'. In order to minimise waste and over-consumption, I believe it makes sense simply to produce only what we need.

Honour the Sacred.

Honour the Earth, our Mother.

Honour the Elders.

Honour all with whom we

share the Earth:

Four-leggeds, two-leggeds,

winged ones,

swimmers, crawlers,

plant and rock people.

Walk in balance and beauty.

Native American saying

American Indians believed in respecting their land too. They believed, also, in taking just what they needed for today, and in giving back. I am not religious, but if I had to choose a religion it would be the same as these Indians: holding Mother Earth as my God, having respect for something real. If all religions worshipped Mother Earth and cared enough not to pollute her, then I believe the world would look very different. We need to reconnect with nature and see that it is something real: very powerful, yet very fragile at the same time.

Imagine what the world would look like if we did consider the needs of the seventh generation hence! How did they get to this belief – so thoughtful, caring and respectful of other generations? The elders commanded a lot of respect from the younger people. They were strict but fair: they made the best decisions for the young and made sure that the future was positive for them. They passed on years of knowledge and wisdom.

The policy of American Indians when they made decisions was to think about how it would affect the next seven generations of their people.

People today – young and old – don't value the lessons of the past. We think that our ancestors knew less than we do, and that with our science we can always do better than them. Certainly, this is true in many cases – but we must also learn what was good about the past, rather than dismissing it to protect financial and political gain.

"The word 'wilderness' occurs approximately 300 times in the Bible, and all its meanings are derogatory."
René Dubois (*The Wooing of the Earth*, 1980)

The Amazon Indians are part of the Amazon's ecosystem. They live now as they did thousands of years ago: in total harmony with nature. It is estimated that there are only about 15 of these tribes left 'undiscovered' in the South American rainforests – they live in such remote places that modern-day humans have yet to discover them. Long may that remain so. If we do come in contact with them one day, we will be able to learn a lot from their basic ways of life, but would we have the humility to do so?

I sometimes think that humankind is like a computer that is slow and corrupt after years of use, full of software and hardware that is not working properly any more. It needs a new operating system installed. Humankind has got too complicated. It could do with a bit of a reset, a software upgrade to a better, more efficient and respectful version of our modern life! We have become slaves of technology, of laws that don't make sense. We need to go back to basics as much as we can, use more common sense in everything we do and not just accept whatever we are given and what we are told.

Earth teach me quiet – as the grasses are still with new light.

Earth teach me suffering – as old stones suffer with memory.

Earth teach me humility – as blossoms are humble with beginning.

Earth teach me caring – as mothers nurture their young.

Earth teach me courage – as the tree that stands alone.

Earth teach me limitation – as the ant that crawls on the ground.

Earth teach me freedom – as the eagle that soars in the sky.

Earth teach me acceptance – as the leaves that die each fall.

Earth teach me renewal – as the seed that rises in the spring.

Earth teach me to forget myself – as melted snow forgets its life.

Earth teach me to remember kindness – as dry fields weep with rain.

Ute Prayer

1.7

NATURE'S RULES

Understanding natural patterns enables us to make good choices

Humankind has not woven the web of life. We are but one thread within it. Whatever we do to the web, we do to ourselves. All things are bound together. All things connect.

Chief Seattle (1854)

◄ *A sunflower is a perfect example of how the patterns in nature can teach us important lessons. When solar panels are erected to reflect the exact spiral nature of the sunflower seed-head, they trap the maximum amount of solar energy available. Nature knew this long before humans did! © Naturefl/Dreamstime*

When I was 17, I first discovered patterns. I went on holiday with my dad for a week, but at that time, I didn't get on that well with him, so I decided to study his patterns of behaviour to find out why. After a while, I was able to predict what he would do and how he would react. With this new understanding, I soon realised that everything was connected to everything else, in a 'web of understanding.' I could subconsciously refer to this and use it to predict what was going to happen! I was amazed at how I could predict things about my dad: it was a powerful feeling for me but I felt sorry for him, as I saw he was trapped in his own thought-patterns. It helped me understand him better. Ever since then I have looked in detail for patterns in everything.

Nature too has patterns and rules that we can follow in order to have a clearer idea of whether a material or product is healthy, green and sustainable. People don't follow the rules of nature because they can't see them, or if they can see them, they don't connect these rules to other aspects of life. Modern life is so complicated that even if we can see the rules we don't know how to interpret them because we have forgotten that all things are connected. But in reality, nothing is that complicated once you strip it down: when you understand the roots you will understand the rest of the tree.

For example if a relationship with someone seems very complex, you could analyse each individual aspect forever and find lots of little solutions. That might make a difference, but at the root of it all is the need to ensure a true respect for each other. When you have this basic respect, everything else will fall into place! Then there will be no need to look at the branches and leaves to solve each problem. Once you have sorted out the root cause the rest will follow – that is the way nature works. If you are stressed then everything bothers you, every last small little thing. If you can get to the root cause of your stress then you relax, and those silly little things disappear, you become more rational, and the peripheral problems around the original stress will sort themselves out. All things are related.

Furniture for the Future by Tristan Titeux

Lakota Instructions for Living

Friend do it this way - that is,
whatever you do in life,
do the very best you can
with both your heart and mind.

And if you do it that way,
the Power Of The Universe
will come to your assistance,
if your heart and mind are in Unity.

When one sits in the Hoop Of The People,
one must be responsible because all of
Creation is related.
And the hurt of one is the hurt of all.
And the honour of one
is the honour of all.
And whatever we do affects everything in
the universe.

If you do it that way - that is,
if you truly join your heart and mind
as One - whatever you ask for,
that's the Way It's Going To Be.

Passed down from White Buffalo Calf Woman

Applying the blueprint to social problems

Illegal drugs are a good example of how society ignores the root causes of social problems. You can arrest drug dealers and imprison them all, but until the root problem is addressed, drugs will always be part of our society. The source of the problem is that people want drugs and create the demand, not the other way around. It is a waste of time to concentrate on the dealer, but by playing piggy-in-the-middle the authorities make it look as if something is being done. But in spite of these apparent efforts, drugs continue to circulate in society. Occasionally rounding up the dealers is a complete waste of time and nothing other than a political game.

We treat crime in the same way: we still put people in prison, as a knee jerk reaction. We don't rehabilitate or educate prisoners properly, we don't get them interested in life, or give them hope. When prisoners are released back into society they go back to the same situation or worse, that sent them into crime in the first place, and so the cycle starts again. They need support on the outside and support on the inside. Throwing people into cells and locking them up is just a waste of resources and completely counterproductive. But perpetuating this cycle is something that can be quantified: statistics can be interpreted in myriad ways and generally used to make it look as if the problem is being dealt with – but we are not dealing with the root cause, we are playing with the branches.

If we look at the patterns behind crime and drugs, we can see that the root causes lie in poverty, poor education, unemployment, lack of aspiration and lack of access to nature. Until these issues are addressed, the criminal patterns of behaviour will continue.

Furniture for the Future by Tristan Titeux

We often hear that simple things are the best, and they are, for the good reason that they work! Human beings over-complicate things: we need to step back and assess the situation as a whole and strip it down. We have too much clutter in our homes and our minds are clouded with unnecessary negative news. I believe we need simpler homes where we can relax and get away from over-consumption and a stressful world and work-life. We would gain from having less, from living a simpler life and considering carefully what we have in order to make sure we don't have too much of what we don't need.

I look at nature and try to understand how and why things work as they do. I know nature has been testing her methods through trial and error for millennia: this is the best kind of test, isn't it? This is real life work-experience based on thousands of years of practice. Nature is wise – she has the best kind of experience and we should consult her wisdom when we want to do something or need answers. We already do this in some ways: many technologies are born from analysing how nature does things and this 'science' is called biomimicry.

> "Nature is just enough; but men and women must comprehend and accept her suggestions."
> Antoinette Blackwell (1825-1921)

We are mystified at how a spider can create a web where each strand is stronger than steel. Researchers have found that the flipper of the humpback whale is a more efficient wing design than the current model used by the aeronautics industry. Similarly, engineers at Airbus have used the rough skin of the shark as inspiration in developing a striated foil coating for the wings of aircraft, a design which has resulted in six percent less friction and improved fuel efficiency. Gecko tape is a product that has been inspired by the lizard's ability to climb up walls and walk along ceilings and mimics the tiny hair-like structures that cover a gecko's feet.

◄ Close-up of green gecko, an animal much admired in biomemtics © C H Baum

Nature has all the answers we need, if only we would look for them

Scientists at the University of Leeds are studying the jet-based defence mechanism of the bombardier beetle to see if the insect can teach them how to re-ignite a gas-turbine aircraft engine in mid-flight. The bombardier beetle is capable of spraying would-be predators with a high-pressure stream of boiling liquid. These are all great examples of biomimetics or biomimicry – the science that uses nature's experience to create modern day solutions that are more in harmony with the earth and more conducive to an efficient and sustainable future.

Natural Parenting

Mother Nature knows what she is doing. She has provided us with milk for our babies since humankind evolved. She is very good at what she does – and then we go and complicate matters! Instead of simply putting a baby to the breast, we decide that this is no good, and give the baby some inert powdered homogenised milk that was designed for a calf to drink. Then we heat it in a bottle and give the baby far too much in one feed because it is easier than heating up 30 bottles a day. This causes digestive problems leading to distress and crying. The baby does not touch the mother's skin or feel the bond. We put our babies in a cage in a separate room because we think that we will smother them if they sleep with us. In nature, animals sleep with their babies; similarly, human babies need to be breast-fed and to go to sleep with the mother as nature intended.

▲ We cannot improve on nature - we are nature.

Nature offers the incredibly complex baby food in a simple way: she has worked out how to give the baby what it needs. The amazing properties of breast milk nourish the baby and adapt according to the particular needs of the baby providing natural immunities at the same time. The act of breast-feeding provides close contact with the mother, and the feel of her skin and the sound of her heartbeat provide security. Sleeping with the baby helps ensure that the parents don't have to endure sleepless nights: the baby wakes and feeds instantly, there is less disrupted sleep and so the mother is better placed the next day to love and cherish her baby.

Humans think that we can improve on this and we fool each other into believing this is true. It is time we used our own common sense and worked with nature and stopped accepting the views of those who just want to make profit: it is not possible to buy the future health that breast milk provides. Look at how nature does things and compare it to what you do: breast milk contains everything that your baby needs, any other milk just won't do the same job, especially if it is pasteurised, homogenised, dried, powdered and non-organic – what life is left in that milk? None compared to the fresh raw milk of a mother.

This is just one example of a root problem and how simple it is to solve. But we don't see the solution because we have let things get complicated and don't understand the nature of our problems. The good news is, we can superimpose nature's map on all our problems from the practical to the emotional: it all works in the same way. Keep it simple, use common sense and whatever you do, observe moderation in all things.

Observe moderation and balance in all things

Furniture for the Future by Tristan Titeux

The beauty of patterns

Patterns recur everywhere in nature and in the universe. They repeat physically, in behaviour and in the mind – even our behaviour as a species has a pattern. In some ways we can be compared to a parasite, because if observed from a distance, humanity is eating away at the rainforest like ants. There are patterns in everything; if you study a pattern somewhere you can see it acting out elsewhere.

If we know that the best, most healthy and nourishing way to eat a cherry is straight off the tree, we can apply this pattern of zero processing to other materials that we use. This is simple stuff, but it is the obvious stuff that we take for granted and don't always think about. These are simple tools but they can be very powerful when you know how to apply them to complex issues.

If patterns occur everywhere it suggests that everything is related – nature is showing us that it uses the same templates in lots different ways and in different places. You can look for a pattern in something you are involved with and compare it to something you have already done. For example, I have decided to specialise in my craft, creating eco-fitted furniture. Why did I do this? Because, I looked at the rainforest and other patterns in nature and saw that in nature insects and plants specialise in order to survive, and that they do so sustainably and in harmony with other ecosystems. So that suggested to me that specialising would be a good thing to do.

You can look at patterns in nature and compare them to your life. You can strip an idea or a project bare like a tree in winter and see how your plans branch here or will eventually produce fruit over there. Everything is connected: if we can understand one thing, we can understand many other things. You don't need to be a specialist! A simple example is that once you understand the power of love and compassion in your life this helps you to makes sense of all relationships, including your relationship with your work, your customers, suppliers, your government, other people, animals, the planet and so much more. If you understand that love and compassion makes good relationships, you can superimpose that pattern onto something else and see that it works there too!

▲ Termites are nature's architectural specialists. Human architects use similar design principles to termite mounds, to naturally ventilate tower blocks. © Sburel/Dreamstime

Patterns of sustainability come and go in cycles: the sun comes up and goes down; the tide goes in and out; our moods go up and down; economies boom and bust; fashion goes around in circles, but every time the cycle repeats it is slightly different. We can predict recessions or at least predict that they will recur. We can be sure that sadly, war too will never end and war in Europe will occur again one day.

Patterns of diversity

▶ *Companion planting benefits from the vitality that biodiversity provides.*

Just to prove that patterns repeat and recycle, I find myself discussing the need for diversity again – but more accurately, the need for patterns in diversity: the best example I can think of for this is micro-finance. A simple system that offers small loans to sole traders and small businesses, it has been found to be so successful – with a 99% repayment rate for those loans – that micro-finance is being replicated all over the world from its humble beginnings in Pakistan. Multiple, small, diverse businesses offer greater financial security than monopolies. Monopolies are not good, they drive up prices, reduce choice and lower working conditions. We need lots of different businesses so people have as much choice as possible. The Competition Commission formally known as the Monopolies and Mergers Commission is supposed to ensure diversity and fair competition. Unfortunately, like many public bodies, they are woven into the fabric of the businesses they are supposed to regulate, and the consumer is the one who loses out. To me, diversification is, beyond question, a good thing.

It is easy to think that we know everything: we see the same things again and again in the news and on television programmes. But the narrow spectrum of the media ignores an undiscovered world of forest gardening, guerrilla gardening and permaculture – these are all solutions to our modern day problems that can be delivered on a small scale, unlike the multinational genetic engineering seed companies that claim to solve our problems. No company with shareholders' interests at heart will save our world. Permaculture mimics the diverse patterns in nature to produce one of the healthiest, most dynamic and productive growing systems ever – so utterly different from the vast monocultures that agribusiness promotes. When did nature ever favour a monoculture?

In business there shouldn't be just one source of income or customer, but a varied and eclectic market. If you rely on one customer base or one source of anything, you're vulnerable. We're realising our vulnerability via uncontrollable petrol prices: we have no choice but to comply unless of course, we take to pedal power. We don't just need one solution such as biofuels or we will have no land left to grow crops. We can't rely on electric cars or hybrid technology as we will be hogging too much of one resource or another. We need to take a balanced view on our use of resources according to how suitable they are to the situation and not according to the market. We have to put sustainability before profit or we will run out of resources, it is that simple. If we choose to ignore this and go against nature, we will pay, not with money, but with human lives.

◀ *This monoculture has to be sprayed with chemicals to ... ... or it lacks the biodiversity to*

1.7.82

Furniture for the Future by Tristan Titeux

We have been going against nature since the start of industrialisation and although that is only about 200 years ago, which is nothing in relation to the history of humankind, and the Earth itself, just look at the mess of pollution and disease we have got into in the last 200 years. It doesn't take much to imagine that if we don't redress the balance in another 200 years, we will be gone! Nature will have the final word for she will live through it as she has with past extinctions.

Recycling is another great example of the diverse patterns in nature that we can learn from. There's no such thing as waste in nature: everything is reused and recycled in myriad incredible ways – isn't that a good idea? Surely that is what we should do, instead of chucking everything into great holes in the ground? It's common sense and we certainly need more of that. If we look at nature we can see that the sea recycles nutrients constantly; every dead leaf in the rainforest is broken down into leaf litter to provide nutrients for new growth. Nothing goes to waste – as soon as an animal dies it goes to feed an amazing variety of different beasts and organisms.

▶ A strawberry embodies the taste of high-summer and pales into insignificance in winter. © Nicophaser/Dreamstime

This tells us that we must be efficient like nature and reduce, reuse and recycle. The more I look at nature's patterns, the more I listen to and study the ways of native peoples, the more I realise how right nature is, how perfect she is and how she knows best and already provides everything we need if we know where to look for it. Nature produces certain foods at certain times of the year, and these things are what are best for us to eat at that time. We must listen to her and not try to produce and eat the same things all the time. Nature is displaying the diversity pattern here again: if you eat the same things all the time it can become toxic to your body.

We are not meant to be eating strawberries for Christmas: they are not that good from the supermarket even when in season, so why would you want to eat these tasteless, watery things in winter? They are a symbol of summer, something to look forward to, as are all fruit and vegetables. The out-of-season varieties are bred for size and selected to be resistant to diseases and to produce lots of fruit. If you take a fruit or vegetable and interfere with its fundamental nature, something will be lost: taste loses out to appearance and price.

Heirloom fruit and vegetables were good, but could not compete in this modern superficial world. The appearance of produce is very important, but it is not the only consideration. You can still get the old varieties of fruit and veg if you look hard for them and some amazing people are nurturing them for us so that we can revert to these varieties if we need to. The Heritage Seed Library is the place in England safeguarding our seeds. So again, variety is key: we need not only strawberries at the right time but also lots of different varieties of them. Apples have around 1200 varieties but commercially we only grow 50. I think it is more than clear that we need variety and lots of it!

Action and Reaction

If a nation gets too big and powerful, over time, things will happen to ensure that it loses its power. Britain once had an empire, as did the Romans. The Greek empire was vast. The USA, once thought invincible, is now losing ground. Life on earth is a jungle, a constant battle for survival. Weeds try to invade other plant space and then a parasite will evolve to control the weeds in some way. These patterns will not stop: we are part of nature however much we fight her and try to believe we are immune. We are weeds in the jungle fighting for our place and nature has her way of controlling us when we push her too much. She reacts to manmade global warming by slapping us with stronger winds, longer rains, endless droughts or frost when the blossoms are in bud.

She is letting us know that she is unhappy: she kills people with diseases and shows us that we are going too far. But it is possible to live happily with nature in symbiosis like the bird that pecks the itchy ticks from the back of the hippo. Whilst nature has ways to punish us when we go too far, she is also there when we need her and she rewards us. We can copy her blueprints and live well – she does not put copyright on her ideas! She is generous and her ideas are 'open source' and patent free. Nature is for all to share, she is not selfish. This is the pattern we should emulate.

"I've been talking to the plants and trees for years now and you'd be amazed at what you can pick up."
The Prince of Wales (2007)

We have amazing people studying different subjects and areas of life, but we need to study in a more holistic way in order to understand the connections between things. There might be someone studying the rainforest, someone studying the seas or someone studying thermodynamics – all of this takes a great deal of time and when studying something in such detail it is hard to see the bigger picture. We need a way to group all these separate strands together more efficiently to be able understand more effectively how all things relate. This would help us be more sympathetic to the fact that we don't act in isolation and that everything we do has an effect on everything else

I believe we have reached the peak of our disconnection with nature and are starting to find ways to reconnect. I am not sure about this, but I am hopeful. I see a lot of good being done, a lot of reparation and with the help of every person on this earth, we can redress the balance and not head into total extinction. We are also part of a cycle: as a baby is born, matures then dies, so does the human race, as do all species. The moons, the stars, and the planets will one day be gone: our sun will age and die as will our own planet. Seen in these terms it is possible to grasp that we are just tiny micro-organisms within the larger universe, which I believe is infinite and has cycles that are infinitely playing out. We have been put on this earth to look after it, so let's get on with it! Let's do the best we can and be as good at it as possible. Let's be kind to our neighbours and our friends. Let's give all we can without holding back.

1.7.84

1.8

THE FUTURE'S GREEN

The forests of the world

I just had to start this chapter on the future of the planet with a eulogy to forests. I love forests, and they really are a fundamental part of humanity's survival on this planet. They are our greatest teachers and providers: they offer us food, shade, building materials; they sequester carbon, stabilise the soil and water and provide for myriad other species. The most important thing any of us can do is to plant trees.

I particularly love the Amazon because, despite severe deforestation, vast areas remain untouched which means we can really see how things would be when left alone. It is just as nature intended: where there is no human interference you can really see nature's patterns. I first learned about the deforestation of the Amazon when I was about 9 years old and the horror of it has stayed with me ever since.

Trees can be replanted but the rainforests can't be replaced. The Amazon has been around for at least 55 million years, but it is estimated that around 200,000 acres of the Amazon rainforest are burned every year. If it carries on at this rate, the Amazon will be gone in our lifetime. How proud will our children be if that happens? It would be a tragedy for us and our descendents (if we have any) because the climate chaos that total deforestation would unleash is likely to be totally devastating.

Experts estimate that we are losing 137 plant, animal and insect species every single day due to rainforest deforestation. That is 50,000 species a year. As the rainforest species disappear, so do many possible cures for life-threatening diseases. Currently, 121 prescription drugs sold worldwide come from plant-derived sources. While 25% of Western pharmaceuticals are derived from rainforest ingredients, less that 1% of these tropical trees and plants have been tested by scientists.

The rainforests are the lungs of the earth.

1.8.88

Deforestation on this scale is a crime against nature and future generations. The Native Americans were all too aware of this and understood that true value in our world is the Earth beneath our feet.

Forests cover one-third of the world's surface; the rainforests now cover 6% of the world's land surface but up until 1950 it was around 15%. An area the size of a football pitch disappears every single second due to deforestation. Clearing the forest to grow mainly soya and cattle, is unsustainable: the value of the Amazon must not be underestimated – it is worth so much more than soya or beef!

When all the trees have been cut down,
When all the animals have been hunted,
When all the waters are polluted,
When all the air is unsafe to breathe,
Only then will you discover you cannot eat money.

Cree Prophecy

The heavens are better understood than the rainforests: astronomers have a better understanding of our galaxy than they do of the numbers of species on Earth. The best estimate puts the number of species at 10 million, and although estimates range from 2 to 100 million, of these only 1.4 million have actually been named. Only 2% of the entire world's surface is true rainforest today, which equates to 6% of the land mass, and yet these forests still support over 50% of the planet's plants and tree species and half of the world's wildlife. Many unknown species are likely to disappear before they have been identified or studied. Over ten years ago the world was warned about the loss of such natural habitats by the eminent biologist and Pulitzer Prize-winner, Edward O. Wilson. Despite his wisdom the destruction goes on and by 2020 it is expected that, if deforestation continues at current rates, almost 90% of rainforest ecosystems will disappear.

We are currently experiencing a mass extinction rate that is unprecedented in over 65 million years

The General Sherman giant Sequoia in Sequoia National Park, California is just one of a few remaining specimens of a forest that once covered the area. Now these magnificent trees are endangered. ▼

GENERAL SHERMAN

The Amazon is not the only forest of significance – the American redwood forests on the East coast of North America are less remote and therefore not so pristine, but have matured for hundreds and thousands of years and cannot be replanted in a hurry! Yet we still use wood from these forests to make paper. What a tragic waste. We should not touch ancient forests, but should be planting sustainable forests for cutting and pulping. 90% of North American virgin forests have already been turned into firewood, shingles, furniture, railway sleepers and paper.

"We abuse land because we regard it as a commodity belonging to us. When we see land as a community to which we belong, we may begin to use it with love and respect."
Aldo Leopold (*A Sand County Almanac* 1949)

Malaysia, Indonesia, Brazil, and other tropical countries with rainforests are seen as the culprits because they are physically destroying their rainforests. But despite the levels of deforestation, up to 60% of their territory is still covered by natural tropical forests. In fact, much of the pressures on their remaining rainforests come from servicing the need for wood products in the industrialized countries that have already depleted their own natural resources.

Industrialised countries would not be buying rainforest hardwoods and timber had we not cut down our own trees long ago, nor would poachers in the Amazon jungle be slaughtering jaguar, ocelot, cayman, and otter if we did not provide lucrative markets for their skins in London, Paris, and New York. It is up to us, the consumers to stop this. I don't think we can blame the people of these countries who are so poor they will do anything to survive. We need to give them other sustainable ways to utilise their land that don't destroy the original forests.

In Canada the boreal forests are also 'old growth'; northern Europe too has lots of old growth forest but still it is cut down. In the UK we still have a very few old growth forests such as Savernake Estate Forest in Wiltshire which is the only private forest in Britain. You can visit it and walk in it freely. Kingley Vale in West Sussex near Chichester, has some of the oldest living organisms in Britain. The trees here are so ancient that other rare organisms have had the time to evolve alongside them. This forest consists mainly of ancient yew trees, some of which are up to 2000 years old.

Windsor forest is designated as a Site of Special Scientific Interest and has oak and beech trees ranging from 300 to 1000 years old and has a unique and internationally-recognised ecosystem. It has more than 2000 species of invertebrates and 1000 species of fungi, many of which are rare or only found in Windsor forest. Sherwood forest contains some of the oldest trees in Europe: veteran oaks five centuries old and the world famous Major Oak, still producing acorns after standing at the heart of the forest for an estimated 800 years. Other forests include the New Forest and Borthwood Copse in the Isle of White. Most trees were cut down in the UK for house and ship building from Roman times onwards so there are very few places where you can still see original forest.

Forests are very productive places: pigs and chickens love foraging in them and many varieties of plants can be found in low density forests, but they are not suited to current large scale methods of production. We need small scale farming operations going on in the forests – it is better to have lots of small farmers working in a cooperative way rather than 2-3 huge farms consuming all the resources and leaving many agricultural workers unemployed.

There are creative ways to mimic natural systems and grow a multitude of crops, with trees, bushes and different types of fruit and vegetables husbanded alongside animals, all in one place, complementing each other, benefiting each other and protecting each other from pests and disease. All the solutions are out there.

1.8.90

If every parent planted a tree for each child, there would be new copses, woods and forests all over the world.

My company, Custom Carpentry, understands how important it is to reforest the land with new trees: not only are they the lungs of the earth and a habitat for a variety of wildlife, our woods and forests are a pleasure to walk through. Any customer of Custom Carpentry that purchases an eco-option gets a tree planted in their name. We also buy sections of rainforest to help safeguard it.

"He that plants trees loves others beside himself."
Dr Thomas Fuller (1732)

▲ Regular walks in woodland are proven to improve mental and physical health. © Socrates/Dreasmtime

3000 fruits are abundant in the rainforests and the indigenous populations use over 2000 of them; but only 200 are in use in the rest of the world.

North America has around seven hundred tree species, but in Borneo more than that can be found in just 25 acres

Rainforest land converted to rearing cattle yields $60 per acre; if the timber is felled it will yield $400 per acre. Should someone decide to nurture and harvest the renewable and sustainable resources, the yield would be $2,400 per acre. By creating a new source of income and harvesting the medicinal plants, fruits, nuts, oil and other sustainable resources, the rainforests are far more valuable alive than slashed and burned. Promoting the use of these sustainable and renewable sources could stop the destruction of the rainforests.

Although Europe's rivers support many species of fish, just one pond in Brazil often supports more.

Approximately half of the estimated 10 million species of animals, plants and insects on the planet live in the rainforests.

Custom Carpentry buys one acre of rainforest on behalf of any customer who takes up an eco-option and places an order worth £5,000. In this way we are helping to save this precious forest from destruction.

The Amazon is home to more species of fish than the whole Atlantic Ocean.

The Amazon basin contains one-fifth of the world's fresh water.

In Peru, one tree was found to host forty-three species of ant, almost equal to the entire ant species of the UK.

Research by the US National Cancer Institute identifies around 3000 plants that are active against cancer cells. 70% of these originate in the rainforests. Organisms from plants found only in the rainforest provide 25% of the active ingredients in today's cancer fighting drugs.

Over 80% of the fruit, vegetables and nuts we eat originated within the tropical forests.

In the future there will be no such thing as 'eco' or green labels – because everything will be green! It will have to be for humanity to survive!

The future will have to be green and sustainable. So why do we not make the change now, before untold damage is done? I recently went to a May Day celebration at a London city farm in the midst of run-down council flats. A boy who couldn't have been more than 7 years old said to his mum: "hey, let's go and have one of their burgers, mum!" Trying to sell the idea, he added, "It's organic – handmade on the farm!" The boy recognised that those attributes were good sales points – enough to use them to try and persuade his mum. I found that amazing! To me it was evidence of the spread of environmental awareness: it's not just people with money now who use words like 'organic,' 'natural,' and 'free range.' On the contrary – many people are instinctively excited by these ideas. And as this young boy showed, you don't need to be an expert in all the tedious arguments about organic certification to act as their 'ambassador'.

The more that people use these words, the more popular and normalised they will become. And this is why I say that in future there will be no such thing as 'eco' or 'green': at some stage, these words will have come to cover everything. It's hard to see arguments about the causes of climate change ending. I strongly suspect that it is down to human actions; others disagree. But we don't need a scientist to tell us that things at the moment are not normal. We can see for ourselves that the world is in a mess.

This spring, my neighbour in Belgium told me that all the flowers came up at the same time, and not at their usual staggered times of year, due to the abnormal heat. I hear stories like that all the time. When usual weather patterns are disturbed, it can have serious consequences on our food crops, as well as on our wildlife (much of which depends for its survival on certain plants growing at certain times of the year).

We have no choice but to be green – but being green is not 'all or nothing'. We don't have to go to extremes. It is possible to be green and have a car for example, if you choose the least polluting model and only use it for necessities. It is possible to be green and go to Spain on holiday, if you go by train and stay in a local farmhouse. You can be green and have nice clothes, if you buy fairly-traded and organic items.

▲ Prototype of hydrogen fuel-cell car designed by Riversimple. © www.riversimple.com

Furniture for the Future by Tristan Titeux

Being green doesn't have to be about wearing sandals and eating lentils (not that I have a problem with either of those things). It's simply about doing our best, making informed decisions and heading in the right direction. It's not about a battle between technology and the Earth – it's about creating technology that is in harmony with the Earth. The ways in which we have used technology have certainly created a lot of harm. But technology is necessary – and it is not going away.

Nor do we want it to. We need technology to get us out of trouble. In the future, sustainable lifestyles will be dependent on good design that makes effective use of technology. I still remember a time about 10 years ago when a friend introduced me as being 'green'. I replied, "it's not that I am 'green'. It's just that you are not 'green' yet!" What I meant by this apparent paradox was that one day, 'green' will become the norm. And when everyone is 'green,' it will make as much sense to refer to someone as being 'green' as to being a 'human being!' We have no choice other than to be sustainable. The alternative to sustainability and renewability is a dead end.

What seems normal now will not be normal in the future. In future, businesses will be green. If they are not, they will be seen as old and 'dirty' businesses. We are living in an uncertain time, when – quite understandably – China, India, African countries, and other nations are aspiring to the level of comfort that the West has become used to. These countries have a choice. They can choose old industries and technologies, which are polluting and ultimately destructive. Alternatively, they can learn from the West's mistakes, leapfrogging our unsustainable ways to create a new green, clean economy. I believe that if they opt for the latter, they will see their standards of living rise significantly above those of over-developed countries such as the UK and the US.

Separating rubbish into its recyclable components means less goes to landfill.
© Baronoskie ▶

The best way to learn is by being encouraged, not penalised. We need to encourage companies and people to be green – rather than discouraging them with penalties, tariffs and subsidies to the polluters. Penalising people (for littering, for example) may work – but only in the short term. In the long term, it makes people resent the government – and the environment. They see being 'green' as something negative. They associate saving the earth with suffering and having less choice. Instead of continuing like this, we need to help people to care more. And for that to happen, people in turn need to feel cared for: they need to see themselves as an integral part of a solution. In my view, if everyone was educated about the reasons for recycling rubbish in a way that developed a sound understanding of the underlying issues, then they would become recyclers through choice.

In any case, positive incentives often work much better than penalties. Imagine if you received money or a gift every time you managed to recycle 80% of your rubbish. Under that scheme, a lot of people would start recycling more. We need to start thinking innovatively about how we can encourage sustainable behaviour,

We are taught as children that if we borrow something, we must take special care of it and give it back. If we break it, we must fix it or replace it. Why did we forget that lesson when we grew up? Many people act responsibly on a personal level, but as a species we seem to have lost our sense of responsibility. We, and those who govern us, need to remember that we have no right to trash the earth.

Why do we think it is okay to throw away rubbish by a stream like this? ▼

The local stream near my house is full of rubbish that has been thrown into it. I often wonder who does this kind of thing. How do people get to a stage where the mind allows that kind of behaviour? It's surely because they see rubbish already there, and therefore know that other people are throwing things away. From there, it's easy to think "everyone else does it," and join in. We need to realise that it is society as a whole that creates this mentality. When we put all our rubbish in giant communal holes, it's almost understandable that people think that it is okay just to throw their rubbish out on the street and into natural environments.

"For the first time in the history of the world, every human being is now subjected to contact with dangerous chemicals, from the moment of conception until death."
Rachel Carson, (*Silent Spring*, 1962)

"We shall require a substantially new manner of thinking if mankind is to survive."
Albert Einstein

Perhaps it is possible to put this kind of behaviour down to irresponsible parenting. Maybe – but the parents have also been brought up in this society of waste, in which we are encouraged to pass responsibility on to other people. We always think that someone else will clean up after us. We need to treat others – and treat nature – as we would treat our children, our parents and our grandparents. That is to say, with total respect: with the sense that we owe them something, rather than that they owe us.

What will our descendants think of us 500 years from now? They will surely think that we were a dirty society. We will be seen as the filthy coal age – the murky, polluted, industrial age. The people of the future are looking back on us just as we now look back at the Middle Ages. We are shocked at how the people used to throw their toilet waste out into the smelly streets. But I am sure the people who lived then just took everything they did for granted, and didn't question their cleanliness – just as we don't question our current unsustainable lifestyles. In the future, things will be cleaner, more efficient, less polluting. That is the picture I have in my mind.

The key to living sustainably in the future is understanding the past. Rather than dismissing everything in the past as old, out of date and unworthy, we should be benefiting from the lessons our predecessors learned through hard experience. We would not be here today had our ancestors not worked so hard to give us all the amazing things we now have: they have a lot to teach us. The best way to learn may be through experience – but studying other people's experiences is also a great way to put one's self on the right track.

Habit and regularity can make pretty much anything seem okay. We tend to accept what we are used to doing and seeing around us. But I also think that we may be reluctant to question what we do because if we did, we would open up a huge can of worms.

The world would look very different if manufacturers were truthful about how they made their products. If we knew where they sourced their materials, who made them (and how they are treated), and how polluting those activities can be, we would surely think carefully before buying their products. But we don't know this, so we accept what we are told.

We furnish and decorate our homes with all manner of artificial materials and we assume that just because someone sells them, these products must be okay. Well, I have news for those who think like that: all most businesses care about is their profit. Many don't know whether their products cause harm – and neither are they trying too hard to find out. Businesses only do test trials on their products when they are made to by external regulatory bodies – and they will often do everything they can to circumvent the rules.

▶ *Milk is not as good for us as we have been led to believe.* © Celwell/Dreamstime

For example, children have been given milk in schools for years, but that doesn't mean milk is good for us: we just assume it is because schools approve of it. But milk is promoted by the dairy industry, and telling us we should drink milk regularly, ensures constant sales. We think of milk as a good source of calcium, but vegetables contain more calcium than milk (and they contain more fibre and are easier to digest.)

A more obvious example of how a combination of habit and corporate lobbying have encouraged acceptance of a harmful product is cigarettes. We now wonder how we could ever have believed that they were not bad for us! And yet for many years we were actually lied to, and told they where good! By whom? By the companies that made them and profited from them.

"You must teach your children that the ground beneath their feet is the ashes of your grandfathers. So that they will respect the land, tell your children that the earth is rich with the lives of our kin. Teach your children what we have taught our children, that the earth is our mother. What befalls the earth befalls the sons of the earth."
– Native American Wisdom

Jamie Oliver (one of my 'food heroes') has been doing great work to help America address its addiction to fast food. This is a country that has gone so far down the dead end track that food isn't really food any more. It's a mass of ingredients concocted in laboratories and factories rather than kitchens. And look how much harm it is doing – soaring obesity rates to name just one side-effect.

▲ Doctors are now warning against a diet consisting mostly of fast foods. © Viorel Dudau

We ingest all sorts of food that contains additives, preservatives, and colourings. We know nothing about these ingredients, but we accept them – supposedly because it makes our food look better and last longer. Those are good enough reasons, according to the people who make these products: but they still don't tell us what those chemicals are. It's simply through habit that we go along with this: we don't question it enough.

"Let me issue and control a nation's money, and I care not who writes the laws."

Mayer Amschel Rothschild

For a long time, we accepted that cars stink and expel a deadly gas. But we eventually got to a stage where we realised that the lead in the petrol was so harmful that we would have to do something about it, and remove it. That was a good step. But what is currently coming out of the exhaust? It is still something deadly and nasty, full of highly dangerous chemicals! How long will it take to get rid of these?

We need to challenge and question what we do, rather than living as passive consumers, feeding the giants who do not care for us, but tell us they do! Big corporations wink at us and we trust them, thinking that because they are in charge, they must know what they are doing, and that they have the best intentions for us. The truth is that they care only about parting us from our money. What hope do we have with people like this running our world?

Cars can now run using the power of the sun. How amazing is that? If you had said that to someone 100 years ago, they would have said that the notion was impossible and that you were crazy – because that was all they knew. So don't think that I'm crazy when I tell you that I believe that one day, cars will be able to run on water. Everything has energy in it, and this energy can be extracted some way. It's just a matter of finding out how.

Furniture for the Future by Tristan Titeux

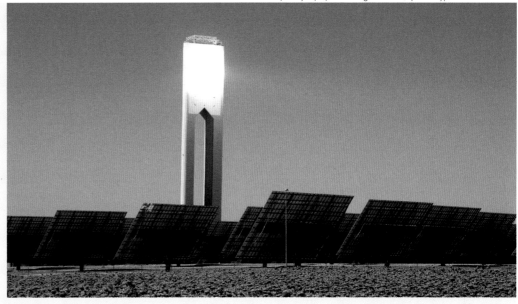

▼ This solar tower collects intensified rays of reflected sunlight in Seville, Spain. © Typhoonski/Dreamstime

"The use of solar energy has not been opened up because the oil industry does not own the sun."

Ralph Nader (1980)

I really think that we can make extraordinary progress over the coming years. Cars and industry will one day run on air. The technology of the future will be able to purify air too, by taking in polluted air and sending it out even cleaner.

I believe that incredible things like this can be possible if we put enough effort and resources into working on them. But sadly, now we encounter a major problem: money. Something will only work if someone can make money from it. So we end up not doing things which a lot of people would support. Because as things currently stand, people don't control what happens. Money, alas – and the few people who own the money – control what happens.

In 2006, 1% of the world's population owned more than 40% of the world's wealth. Think about what that means. It means that if you want to do anything serious, you have to get these people in on it. And if they are involved with a competitor to water and air-based energy – like oil or electricity – then that is going to be hard to do. We all instinctively want to preserve ourselves, and if something threatens us and our life, we fight it off. Science is relatively easy to predict – you can work it out like maths. But humans are harder to understand, so really I can't predict if the human race will be able to overcome this difficulty. But I sincerely hope that we will overcome it.

I believe that most of us are not evil – not even the richest of the rich that rule the world. Once these people realise that they too can benefit from cars that run on water, then they will play ball. But don't forget that there will never be one single solution. It's easy to start thinking that sea water or air could be the one ultimate solution – but nature says that won't work! In order to use our resources sustainably, we need many different solutions. Otherwise, the next thing we know, we will be emptying our oceans and causing permanent rain – or creating some other disaster!

We are at the beginning of an exciting journey that will take us places we don't yet know and can't even imagine. The idea of a water-powered car might seem radical – but perhaps the most radical thing about it is that in the grand scheme of things, it is really not that radical at all!

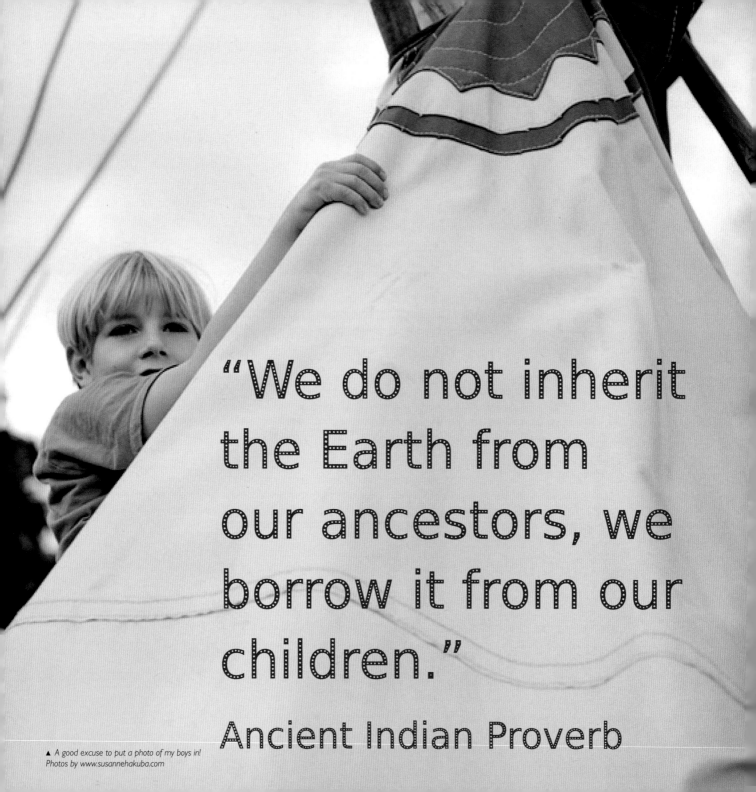

"We do not inherit the Earth from our ancestors, we borrow it from our children."

Ancient Indian Proverb

▲ A good excuse to put a photo of my boys in!
Photos by www.susannehakuba.com

2.1

FROM DREAMS TO REALITY

The philosophies and practitioners of good design

My Dreams for a Sustainable Future

To me, the ultimate aim for all production processes is for materials to be grown, used, then composted or burned in houses directly for heating, not in inefficient power stations, although this could work as an interim measure instead of fossil fuels. Just picture in the future that at the end of the useful life of your cupboard, printer or even your car, you can put whatever item it is straight onto the compost pile to rot away, or to the local power station to burn, or even better, take it to the recycling centre and come back the next day when they have transformed it all into pellets that you can burn in your own fire or purpose-built heating system.

This might seem a little crazy because you may think, you can't burn or compost glass, or an engine, or tyres! Well no, not as they are now, but just remember that the bodywork of the first cars ever produced was made from hemp fibre which is compostable, and that glass is made from natural materials. Just imagine that it is actually possible to make the glass out of a burnable or compostable material that releases no more chemicals into the air than that of burning wood, or imagine that the engine of a vehicle is made from a super-efficient plant-based material, or that tyres are totally biodegradable – why not? We have the technology and the resourcefulness – and as finite resources become ever more scarce, we will need to find ways to reuse, recycle and remake.

Furniture for the Future by Tristan Titeux

I find it helpful to envisage what the ultimate in anything is: what could be the best case scenario and the worst case scenario? A car that is totally nontoxic to its users, that is totally burnable or compostable and that harms the environment no more than burning wood is the pinnacle of sustainability and the best case scenario. Our designers should aim for that, so that we don't have to endure the worst case scenario that we currently have.

So, now that I have stated what I believe to be the pinnacle of sustainable design, we can see how close to that goal we are in everything we do. I use the car as an example because I actually love cars – or at least what they can do for us. They enable us to get around fast without getting wet and cold, to meet friends and family or to transport heavy goods. Some people are so against the car, but if a car was totally recyclable and used zero-emission power (such as solar electricity), then what could people have against it? I believe we can one day achieve this ultimate car and I really do believe that we can make almost anything from plants and natural materials.

There are many millions of working cars on this earth and around 50 million new cars every year being produced. Imagine how many resources would be saved by totally recycling every car! In fact, the car industry is one of the most efficient industries at recycling and reusing products. In the UK 85% of a car by weight must be recycled, reused or recovered, and by 2015 the aim is for 95%. That is amazing progress! Car manufacturers have tough targets to meet: it's about time the construction industry came up to the same standards.

It's all about good design: if packaging were designed to biodegrade, we could easily reduce our landfill problems; if household goods were reusable, repairable and recyclable, not only could we create meaningful jobs but also significantly reduce our impact on the environment. It's worth stating again that many of the problems we face could be solved with good design.

"I have no doubt that we will be successful in harnessing the sun's energy... If sunbeams were weapons of war, we would have had solar energy centuries ago."
Sir George Porter

Your Beautiful Home

Expert advice on how to make the right choices for a healthy home

Your house is more than just bricks and mortar – it is your place of sanctuary, somewhere you can express your creativity and say a little about who you are and what motivates you. Some homes are full of celebrity memorabilia; some homes are full of antiques – this says so much about the people who live there. I like my home to be full of natural materials, recycled and upcycled products and mindful purchasing decisions. This is because I care about the future of the planet and want to set a good example to my children, friends and family. Out of interest, I asked some leading advocates of eco-design and sustainable living what items they like to have in their homes, and why we should choose natural, sustainable and eco-friendly materials.

Emma Phelps

Design Director at 20age

I work by upcycling and redesigning vintage, classic furniture, so the idea of being 'eco' in the home is of great interest and importance to me. The concept of taking something old to create something new can be inventive and exciting as well as being environmentally sound. Do we really need to always buy new when a lot of the old classic designs were made expertly to last? Reinvention can be just as interesting as new design - recycling a used and loved piece to create something new is eco friendly and I know that I personally would rather use items in my home that help and save our environment rather than hinder it.

◄ *Upcycled Feira De Santana armchair, by Emma Phelps. © Emma Phelps*

"Who needs the new when you can rediscover the old!"
Emma Phelps, Design Director at 20age

Denise Portmann and Ladina Hardmeier

Designer-makers and founders of Studio180°

With the growing green movement, there is a rising demand for products and services in the field of eco-design. True eco-friendly products are made from non-toxic materials that do not harm humans or the environment. Natural materials have many excellent properties: for example, carpets and fabrics made from wool can purify indoor air for up to 30 years and remove noxious gases without releasing them, as well as regulating humidity in interior spaces. Innovative eco-materials and fresh contemporary designs enable a creative approach to green interior design, and the crafting of beautiful, eco-homes.

"Choosing sustainable and eco-friendly materials for your own home adds an important element to healthy lifestyles and well-being."

Max McMurdo

Eco-Designer and MD of Design Consultancy
Reestore

'Silvana' – once a washing-machine drum, now a beautiful floor light, by Max McMurdo. © Max McMurdo ▼

"Sustainability in the home can be achieved on a number of levels and really doesn't have to cost a fortune."

I don't expect everyone to be sitting at home in my handmade shopping-trolley chairs or bathtub sofas! But, design classics such as Ercol and G Plan can be scavenged from junk shops – you'll be gaining well-made items that are built to last while preventing them from going to landfill. Bookshelves can be made of breezeblocks or bricks painted white, with glass sourced from an office refurbishment at no cost – and they look great. Or, how about the occasional washing-machine drum table with built-in light to add to the atmosphere! And why not buy second-hand kitchen units, or reuse your old ones; simply paint the doors a contemporary colour and replace the work surfaces with some solid local wood to give it a new lease of life.

Claire Danthois

Reclaimed-Furniture Designer and Creator Of The Award-Winning 'Once A Door' Chair

"By spending a little time on choosing your furniture more thoughtfully, you will end up with a much richer and more varied interior that is different from anyone else's."

I believe you should consider the durability of the furniture you buy, investing in something that will last and that has a special meaning to you. This is the concept on which I base my work and it's why I choose to keep some of the material's original quality visible … telling a story of its past existence, giving an item of furniture more depth. Of course financially it's not always possible to do this with every item in your home, but if you have just a few pieces like this you can play with combinations of old and new, modern/contemporary and classic/antique. Choosing materials that are sustainable and durable should become second nature to people. Looking after our planet and the environment are fundamental considerations and the more the consumer demands these, the more the industry will have to produce sustainable products. Until such time it's up to us as consumers to seek out designs that are ecologically sound.

Once a Door', by Claire Danthois made of recycled timber taken from an old door © Claire Danthois ▶

Sarah Turner

Eco Art & Design

"Just because a product is made from waste materials, doesn't mean it needs to look like it does!"

Of course it is important for our environment to buy eco-consciously, but also if you have items in your home made from eco-friendly materials then you will feel proud to own these things: proud that you made an eco-friendly choice and you will remember their origins whenever you look at them. I think that often people's perception of eco-friendly or recycled products is that they might be a compromise on style or quality. I hope that products such as my own disprove this point.

Sarah with her collection of lampshades made from recycled plastic bottles. © *Sarah Turner* ▲

Furniture for the Future by Tristan Titeux

Julia Kendell

Interior Designer, TV Presenter (DIY SOS &
60 Minute Makeover) and contributor to Real
Homes magazine

"My passion is to inspire people to live an exciting life, responsibly and
ethically. I eschew packaging and unnecessary consumerism and I am on
a mission to encourage people, particularly ladies, to learn trades and
skills."

When buying for your home I believe it is imperative to make choices based on sound principles, such as value, longevity, provenance and sustainability. Over the past few decades it has been all too easy to buy on a whim, with little regard for where a product has come from and at what cost to local communities and the planet, but these days we are far better informed. I hope this greater awareness, combined with old-fashioned values of buying the best you can afford and mending when necessary, will start to lessen the impact of our consumerism. After all, buying 'eco' does not confine you to a life of sackcloth and string!

William Lana

Co-founder of Eco-Textiles company
Greenfibres

Most people lead busy lives and it's not easy to make every purchase a mindful one. But imagine if just one in five of our decisions could be ethically driven. That would be £150 billion pounds a year going towards products and services that are solution focused. On our garment labels we use the phrase 'What you buy will be produced, what you don't won't.' At the end of the day, what's the point of having all this choice if we don't exercise it to make the world a better place?

In the UK, consumers spend approximately £750 billion a year. What we choose to spend this money on makes a huge difference. Assuming we accept that not all products and services are equal, the first decision we need to make as consumers is 'I want to try to spend my money ethically.' If we support a service that brings a community closer together or if we buy a product that is ethically made from natural and organic raw materials – that makes a difference.

"Leave everything
you touch a bit more
beautiful."

Ptolemy Elrington

Possibly The Best Hubcap Artist In The World

I think it is of the utmost importance that we factor-in reuseable or recyclable materials in the home, and the use of eco-friendly materials is a given. The problem of our ever-growing world population and increasingly limited resources is a common discussion topic and it's ludicrous to ignore this any longer. This means not only preparing for the future but treating our environment with respect right now. Our children need us to take these actions — and take them immediately.

Fantastic fish made purely from plastic car hubcaps found in the street. © Ptolemy Elrington ▲

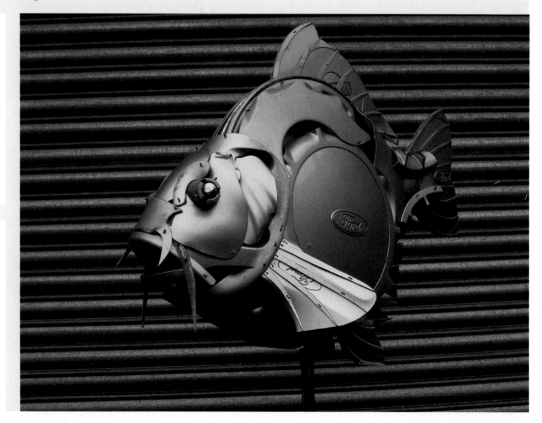

"I have come across many things which have been abandoned and find something more in them than their intrinsic worthlessness."

Furniture for the Future by Tristan Titeux

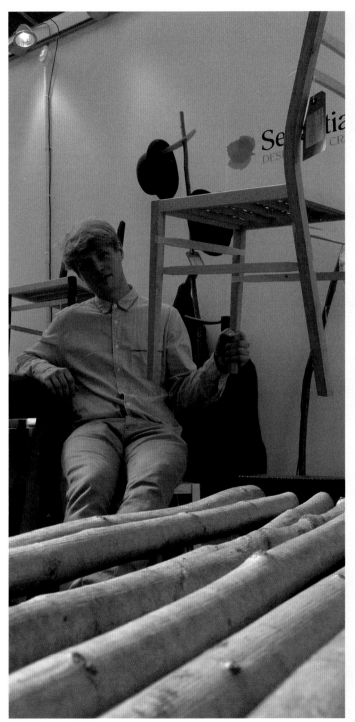

Sebastian Cox

Furniture Maker

I make sustainable furniture from fast growing hazel wood coppiced from the British countryside. Hazel is a bit like bamboo in the sense that it grows fast, grows in clumps, straight up into nice straight sticks that can be cut at the bottom allowing the hazel to naturally regenerate. This process is call coppicing. There's no need to cut a tree down and replant another and disturb the ecosystem of the soil in the process – which is one of the reasons why I love to work with coppiced wood. A hazel copse can be managed by rotating the cutting process and extraction of wood from one area per year to another, until 8 years later you get back to where you started with the new growth ready to harvest. This is how hazel was traditionally managed. Every year I organise a little party of friends and we go into the wood and cut a whole year's supply. I am fortunate to be able to sell my furniture in the prestigious Liberty store in London's Regent Street. I also won Kevin McCloud's Green Hero's award for my work promoting hazel as a sustainable wood.

"Go for sustainably-sourced wood wherever possible."

◄ *Sebastian Cox holds up one of his ultra-light, sustainable coppiced hazel chairs.*

Maddy Harland

Editor of Permaculture Magazine

"I will never forget seeing a friend's coffin. He was a permaculture designer who died tragically young. His family cremated him in finest mahogany with brass handles, unaware of the ecological implications. I didn't have the heart to say anything but my friend would have preferred a more modest willow or softwood coffin."

I avoid buying manufactured goods made from formaldehyde, fire retardants, volatile organic compounds, PVC or other materials that off-gas toxic fumes during their lifetime. We care far more about organic and natural foods and yet we often ignore the potential toxicity of the materials we bring into our homes. I also need to know the origins of the materials that make up my furniture. If they are from old-growth deciduous forest or from tropical hardwoods that are irreplaceable remnants of biodiversity in their bioregion, for example, then for me cutting the trees down it not an option. It's relatively easy to identify FSC-certified products and check the status of the timber used. So, 'cradle-to-grave' costs, chemical toxicity, aesthetics and ethical reasons all come into play and have to be balanced with finances.

For me, there are many reasons for choosing eco-materials and quality crafted products. Whenever possible I prefer to buy a handmade item that will last not only my lifetime but the lifetimes of my children and beyond. Apart from the environmental implications of buying something cheap and throwing it into landfill when it breaks, there is great pleasure in the feel of a crafted piece made with time and care by a skilled artisan. So if I can afford to, I'd rather invest in a quality product and have the pleasure of it for years than buy one of dubious provenance with a short lifespan.

Furniture for the Future by Tristan Titeux

Orapin Sinamonvech

Founder and CEO of KokoBoard

To address many of the environmental problems we face, we recommend the development of social enterprises that create green products and jobs which benefit not only the customer but also the environment, and the community producers. Kokoboard is an example of one such social enterprise, based in Thailand. We started with the idea that we wanted to help raise incomes for farmers by adding value to agricultural residues. We did this by developing technological know-how to transform agricultural wastes into bio-particleboards (similar to MDF but without formaldehyde). This helps reduce deforestation and extends the life of living green forest for future generation. Our mission is to develop technology to suit local communities and transfer the know-how to make bio-particleboards to other regions in Thailand. Our current products are rice straw board, coconut dust board, grass board, peanut shell board and sunflower board.

A Kokoboard dividing wall, made from coconut dust fibre. © Orapin Sinamonvech ▶

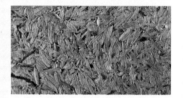

"KokoBoard is an alternative choice for wood lovers, while helping to reduce air pollution and carbon dioxide emissions."

Henry Swanzy

Understorey: Contemporary, Sustainable
Designers

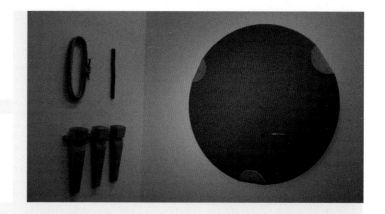

"As designers it is our responsibility to create objects that reflect a growing understanding of finite natural resources. My ethos is one that aims to rediscover value in materials that are locally produced and whose management systems are understood.

A piece of furniture made locally, from responsibly-sourced materials, has a smaller carbon footprint than one that needs to be shipped halfway across the world – but more important than that, it contains a message: it says that we are aware, and that we care. In a world of ubiquitous global brands, design that is from, and of a certain place is a chance to express our individuality and reflect our cultural heritage."

"I don't think we should be under any illusions: eco-friendly furniture isn't going to save the planet! But it can make a little difference, and lots of little differences make big ones."

Henry from Understorey with his 'Peg-leg Table.'
© Understorey ▶

Furniture for the Future by Tristan Titeux

Paul Firbank
The Rag and Bone Man

Paul Firbank is a designer-maker of furniture and lighting who has an admiration for things that were built to last, which is why he reincorporates scraps of industrial history and end-of-life vehicles and machines into his new work. On the importance of using eco-friendly materials in the home:

▲ Photo © Ellie Laycock

"In terms of interiors I like to think about what an eco-friendly approach can add to the home. For me recycling and repurposing is a way to be resourceful and save money, and it's an opportunity to enrich a home with pieces that tell different stories through their past and new applications. I prefer to spend my money on vintage machine parts which were beautifully designed and built to last and repurpose these elements into something new, rather than buy a modern mass-produced item that has a guarantee of 2 years. It's just having the vision to see a new life in something. In doing this you will also have a unique piece that can be a real feature in the home."

Katy Brice and Adam Weismann

Founders, Clayworks

We are strong proponents of using not just eco-friendly materials in the home, but also natural materials. By this, we mean simple materials derived from nature that are as unadulterated from their natural source as possible. Into this category fall materials made up of earth (clay), stone, wood, and mineral and vegetable matter. We believe these natural materials enhance our lives for a number of reasons. We are ourselves 'natural' beings made up of the elements of nature. When we live around natural materials in our homes, we tend to create an ambience of harmony. Our homes become an extension of the outside. Natural materials tend to be porous, which means they 'breathe'. This has a positive effect on the way moisture is managed in a building and reduces the potential for negative microbial activity in the home, such as dust mites, as well as creating the most comfortable air for our human mucus membranes.

Detail of a house built and furnished using natural materials including cob, clay, slate and stone. © Clayworks ▲

▲ *Clay doesn't have to mean rustic*

Natural materials generally have a much lower overall embodied energy during their full life cycle. This means they contribute to less use of energy during their production, how they behave once in use, and how they biodegrade at the end of their life cycle. Many, such as clay, can even be recycled back into the system with relatively little energy. Natural materials are free from artificial and dangerous chemicals, solvents and VOCs (volatile organic compounds). In a time when there is a growing trend to create air tight buildings to mitigate heat loss, it is even more important to use materials that will not create an internal toxic soup – potentially dangerous for all life forms.

"Natural materials are beautiful to look at and be around. They are healthy for people (and all life forms), the planet and buildings."

Zoe Murphy recycles stylish old quality retro furniture with her own beautiful hand printed designs inspired by the 1930s and 50s. © Zoe Murphy ▶

Zoe Murphy

Designer and Upcycler

"I have always promoted the idea 'love what belongs to you.' I enjoy printing onto recycled furniture and textiles using imagery inspired by my seaside hometown. I find the use of print and craft to be a very effective way to draw attention to something that had previously lost value. Getting people to reconnect with their objects is incredibly important to me."

I consider the quality and environmental responsibility of products to be every bit as important as the aesthetic. Everyone has been made aware that as a species we are consuming at levels that cannot be sustained in the long run. If we want future generations to be able to live in any way that they choose to, and not be restricted by the environmental costs of our current way of life, we need to start looking very carefully at how we produce and buy things. These sorts of decisions can come in the form of buying less and spending more carefully, or using our spending power to invest in more eco-friendly materials in the home - ones that limit their damage to the planet. These sorts of decisions aren't just relevant to those who will follow us: the way we spend can also have a direct impact on the living conditions of people in different parts of the world today. Taking a good look at an item you are about to buy, and asking questions like 'how was this made?' 'who made this?' 'how were they treated?' and 'what is the impact of these materials?' is important. We are not just isolated consumers, we are part of a system, and should recognise that our demand makes us responsible for all of the others that precede and follow us in the chain.

2.2

MATERIALS AND DESIGN

Fitted furniture can be incredibly wasteful if it is not thought through properly. People often move into a house, rip everything out and start again from scratch. As a result, I often see entire kitchens and bathrooms out on the pavement or in skips around Notting Hill in London. It breaks my heart to see all this stuff being dumped when it could be reused. Surely there should be a recycling centre in every neighbourhood where everything gets taken to, sorted and redistributed, as a matter of course?

"Waste is a tax on the whole people."
Albert W. Atwood

◄ We are an incredibly wasteful society: all this 'waste' is actually valuable resources.

I want to avoid my fitted furniture ending up in a skip. I want it to be designed so that it is beautiful and timeless, made with attention to detail using quality materials. Classically-designed furniture never goes out of date – clean and simple lines complement any style of house and furnishings. Good design will ensure that when the furniture does run its course, it can be easily removed and reused.

Furniture should do exactly what the customer wants – but also be flexible, so it can be put to many uses. Time spent in consultation and planning means is time well spent.

"For 200 years we've been conquering nature. Now we're beating it to death."
Tom McMillan (Francesca Lyman, The Greenhouse Trap, 1990)

In 2004, the building industry produced around 100 million tonnes of landfill waste. This is more than three times the amount of domestic waste collected (28 million). It is estimated that each year, households produce up to 420,000 tonnes of waste wood. Packaging (such as pallets and crates) produces a further 670,000 tonnes, and construction and demolition 750,000 tonnes, according to DEFRA.

These are huge amounts – but it's partly because of this that there is great potential to do something about this situation. When people are doing up a whole house, there are all kinds of administrative hoops they have to jump through – and while I don't want to add more bureaucracy into the equation for the sake of it, the planning and permit stage would be a good time to work out a simple plan for capturing and reusing all that material. The government, or social enterprises, could come and pick up the unwanted waste so it can be reused and recycled.

▲ Bookshelves designed to make the most of an underused space. © Custom Carpentry

Furniture for the Future by Tristan Titeux

"To waste, to destroy our natural resources, to skin and exhaust the land instead of using it so as to increase its usefulness, will result in undermining in the days of our children the very prosperity which we ought by right to hand down to them amplified and developed."
Theodore Roosevelt

We need to establish some rules as to what can be done to materials, and in what order. For example, we mustn't burn straw and chipboard to produce energy when they can still be used to make things. Once a product has been used for its first intended purpose, then it should be reused. If that is not possible, then it should be recycled. And only if that isn't possible should the material be composted or burned (presuming that it is not toxic, of course). This philosophy will work better if natural materials are used, which are easier to reclaim, reuse and recycle. The right solution needs the right materials.

▲ The ultimate in reuse! Plastic bottles are tied to a fence, filled with soil and used to grow salad crops. © LowFm6510

But the principle that should come even before 'reuse' is 'reduce.' We need to reduce the amounts of what we use, what we throw away, and what we buy. Before we buy anything, we need to think twice about whether we really need it, whether it is it the best quality, and whether it will last.

An everyday example of 're-use' is the milk bottles that were traditionally left on the doorstep to be collected. Cleaning them out and filling them up again with milk is a much better option than smashing them up in order to melt them and make into new bottles – which is very energy intensive. In Europe, it is still pretty standard to reuse bottles in this way for many things – such as beer and juice.

So – use less in the first place, and think and plan your purchases with the long term in mind. Buy goods that use minimal packaging, and request that the packaging be natural or recyclable. When you're done with something, give it away on Freecycle or Junk Sniper; sell it cheap at a car boot sale, or donate it to charity. Give toys to your local play centre, and books to your library – and lend a whole range of stuff to other people using sites like Ecomodo or The Borrowers.

Some great companies are already collecting and recycling a lot of waste. In 2010, AnyJunk sent 12 tonnes of textiles to Oxfam – that's equivalent to 63,000 T-shirts. 31 tonnes of books and 187 tonnes of furniture and bric-a-brac (equivalent to 4,675 sofas) were also reused, and 540 tonnes of wood (equivalent to 77,000 wooden chairs) were directly recycled. 704 tonnes of metal and non hazardous electrical waste were recycled or refurbished, as were 56 tonnes of TVs and computer monitors, fridges and fluorescent tubes. AnyJunk and Eco Rubbish Clearance also recycled 551 tonnes of rubble and inert waste, as well as 59 further tonnes of other materials.

There is also a social enterprise specialising in wood collection called The National Community Wood Recycling Project. They pick up and recycle your wood and resell it – and also help people start up their own wood recycling enterprises. That's something I would love to do!

Eco-Furniture Options

Eco-furniture is made of natural materials that are easy to turn into something else, or which can later be recycled, reused, composted or burned safely.

Freestanding furniture is generally more sustainable than fitted furniture because it can be moved from house to house and is not dependent on a particular space. And it's especially sustainable if it is made solidly of the right quality durable materials, and is of long-lasting timeless design. I work with many eco companies that can produce freestanding furniture made from local English wood.

The most sustainable solution for existing furniture is simply reusing it. The longer you can keep your furniture living, the less you will be throwing away. So think about something before you buy it – and when you are bored of it, give it away or sell it. And before you decide you don't want something any more, remember that you can bring it back to life with some paint, or sand it down and refurbish it. We work with restorers who can revive and transform your furniture.

These principles also apply to fitted furniture. If you have white fitted furniture that has been hand painted (not spray-painted, a method which currently uses very toxic paints) such as we do, you can easily freshen it up with a new coat of paint. This can be done again and again, to make your fitted furniture like new. Since fitted furniture has a limited life, the best materials are those that can either be composted or recycled or reused into something else.

Chipboard for fitted furniture can now be made from all sorts of raw materials including rice straw, nut shells and bamboo. ▼

At the moment, petrochemical-derived glues are used in making chipboard, MDF and plywood. I look forward to the day when these materials are made using natural glues. Ideally, a new process to bind the fibres naturally will eventually negate the use of glues. I believe that we humans have the ingenuity to make something close to that possible.

When putting in fitted furniture, you should also use quality hardware that will last: stainless steel handles are infinitely recyclable and made of recycled material. And demand quality hinges, so that the doors stay on. See Pioneering Projects on page 2.3.136 for more practical ideas on how to make fitted furniture more long-lasting and flexible. Different combinations of innovative thinking, techniques and materials can make fitted furniture an eco-friendly option for your home.

Quality and Durability

If you are going to have fitted furniture made, it has to be right the first time. Otherwise, you will have to pull it out and spend money again. So it's better to spend a bit of time searching for someone who will do the best job for you, and who cares about creating beautiful designs. You'll see that eco fitted furniture can be beautiful, durable, good quality and flexible.

Durability is about using the right material for the job in hand. It isn't so much about the material but about how it is used. I have seen a lot of problems with furniture that are caused by bad design. The shelves bow because the wood is too thin, the doors fall off because there aren't enough hinges. People will call my company to see if we can help, complaining that the furniture they have bought elsewhere is poor quality and the finishes are rough.

Custom Carpentry, my furniture-making business, makes furniture fit for its purpose. It will stay up, look good and be properly finished – with smooth, sanded edges, rather than jagged ones. I hear a lot about (and see a lot of) cheap finishes: unrounded edges, saw-marks and so on. I am fully aware that these problems are all too common – but Custom Carpentry is not responsible for any of them, because the company values good design and attention to detail. If furniture has been poorly finished, the customer will want to replace it after a while – and this makes it more unsustainable.

◄ *Custom Carpentry makes high-quality, durable fitted furniture.*

The time spent getting a good finish takes as long as the rest of the bulk of the work – but it's worth it, because at the end you have something beautiful, and beautiful furniture will last forever. It will cut through culture, fashion and time – and is more sustainable for that reason. Things that come into fashion soon fall out of fashion, so it is best to stick to simple design. I mean simple in a positive sense, though. 'Simple' rarely means 'cheap.' To create something truly simple is more difficult than making something highly ornate. With something simple and plain, there is nowhere to hide any flaws. A molehill is much easier to spot on a super-flat lawn than in a meadow full of plants!

Quality brings satisfaction. When you own something that is well made, solid, and works well, it makes you feel good. Something cheap takes its toll on your mind – it bothers you, it makes you wish you had bought something that was better quality. At Custom Carpentry, we understand that. 'Cheap' is not part of what we do. If you can afford it, quality is worth doing – because you get so much more satisfaction from something well-made.

Intelligent design is an important part of what we do too. We think about what clients want to use their furniture for – and we prompt them to think of things that they might not have thought of themselves. We ask them questions and fully involve them in the design process, so that they can let us know exactly what they want.

If you order fitted furniture from us, we will measure your belongings to see how everything fits. Then we will think about what else you might want to use your furniture for in the future. If you have a baby, you may want to turn your office into a nursery, for example – or later, you may want to do the opposite. In this instance, we might give you the possibility of being able to easily add rails, or adjustable shelves that can be moved around to suit new uses.

We also want you to think about whether you would want to sell your house, and if so, how your fitted furniture could add value to it. You can use it as a talking point when showing people around!

Furniture for the Future by Tristan Titeux

Benefits of natural, renewable materials

The benefits of natural materials are many and varied. They are cheaper, because natural materials require little processing and little energy to transform them from their original state. Straw, for example, is a waste material worth very little in monetary terms. If you used straw bales from the field to build your house, you could have them for as little as 80 pence each. Then it would simply be a matter of stacking them up! Of course, making strawboard requires a factory and that in turn requires energy. But the principle remains the same: the less processing a material needs to go through, the cheaper it can be.

▲ Straw has a great future in eco-furniture as a raw material for fibreboard products.

Many natural materials can be grown or sourced locally. Locally-produced materials need less transport, and often don't rely on oil wells in foreign lands with uncontrollable prices. Straw, hemp, and flax can be grown in many places. Or you can even just dig earth and clay from the ground to build walls using rammed-earth techniques.

Natural materials are also healthier because they are less processed. Paints made with plant materials, for example, don't contain highly toxic chemicals like traditional paint does. Unfortunately, while it is possible to get MDF (Medium Density Fibreboard) made without formaldehyde, I wouldn't exactly call the new version healthy!

My ultimate aim in being an ambassador for natural materials is to encourage people to demand solutions and better products. Hotels and offices around the world use composite board such as MDF to make their fitted furniture. Instead of telling people that they can't use it, I would rather encourage the transformation of the industry. We need materials like MDF. They can be incredibly sustainable, and companies are already creating innovative new versions. One new type of MDF, for example, is extremely durable and uses a totally clean manufacturing process called Tricoya.

Natural materials often work better, but again it all depends on the situation. You need to use the right thing for the right purpose. This is a theme that runs through everything. Why use metal to build roof structures when we can use wood? But we can't use wood yet to make car engines, so use the metal for that!

According to the US Geological Survey, most metals have fewer than 100 years left before they become depleted at source. We should use metal only where nothing else will do. Other materials are often superior: wood, for example, can be used in many instances instead of metal. Wood is a renewable resource – metal is not.

This beautiful wooden table, hewn from a single tree trunk will last for years and is more sustainable than a metal equivalent.

Wood is better to use than metal because it doesn't affect the natural electromagnetic fields around your home. Wood is better to use than plastic because it doesn't give off poisonous fumes and doesn't pollute the environment through its manufacture. Natural paint does not pollute your living environment with unnatural chemicals. It makes sense to use materials that work in line with nature.

Clay is an incredible natural material. When the room becomes too dry, clay naturally regulates the environment of your home and keeps it at the optimal level that is healthy for the human body. If a company had invented something similar to clay, they would be promoting it as amazing space age technology! It can also, to some extent, absorb VOCs (volatile organic compounds) and other pollutants. It makes humidity levels sufficiently low that dust mites and mould are unable to spore. Its thermal mass also helps regulate fluctuations in temperature as well as humidity.

▲ *A selection of natural raw materials and pigments for eco-paints. © Auro*

Furniture for the Future by Tristan Titeux

This is not meant to be an exhaustive list of available sustainable materials, but rather a selection of some of those that I have come across and I am particularly interested in. We have used some of these ourselves, and there are many interesting facts and stories about them.

The ultimate reference library of over 1,200 materials that either come from renewable resources or use less non-renewable resources can be found at the 'Rematerialise' Library at Kingston University in London. Other excellent sources of information are SCIN Gallery in Old Street, London - which holds exhibitions, The Building Centre, and the Material Lab.

Eco-Materials Suitable For Fitted Furniture

Strawboard

Strawboard is great as it uses a waste product that grows quickly, and isn't taking up land that could otherwise be used to grow food. If grown organically, it is very sustainable. Currently, strawboard isn't organically certified, and standard strawboard isn't made in the UK yet. Most strawboard comes from China, so shipping it for use in the UK drastically reduces its sustainability, but there's no reason why it should not be produced here. Strawboard is formaldehyde-free and uses an MDI-type glue. This is the least hazardous form of glue because it doesn't contain formaldehyde, but only time will tell how bad this one is. The glue is still derived from petrochemicals, but again, further research into the subject should enable a more benign product to be made.

Detail of a strawboard shelf, with edges left ragged to show the raw materials it is comprised of. ▼

"When some high-sounding institute states that a compound is harmless or a process free of risk, it is wise to know whence the institute or the scientists who work there obtain their financial support."
The Lancet, 1973

There is one kind of strawboard grown and produced in the UK – Stramit. The great thing about this is that it contains no glue to hold the straw together. The usual strawboard described above is like chipboard – ground up straw. The Stramit strawboard, however, uses whole clumps of straw, which means that it is less processed. It is pressed at incredibly high pressure, making it very dense. The board is around 58mm thick, and the only place where glue is used is on the outside to bond art paper that clads it and keeps it together.

We are the first fitted furniture company to be mad enough to use this material in furniture – it is normally used for house building and insulation. But I don't see boundaries in materials. I prefer to use my imagination to think how a material can be used, as opposed to how a material can't be used. I don't listen to those who say "that won't work!" I know in my mind what I want to do and I like to learn and experiment.

◄ Straw shelves in pioneering project "Stram Straw" designed by Tristan Titeux

I talk more about this strawboard in my Pioneering Projects section. You can't get much more natural than wood and straw. Notwithstanding the glue, it is a fantastic product. It can be made into large sheets of material 3 meters long and over and up to 2 meters wide. It is very versatile because it is flat and can be cut into any size you need – its uses are infinite.

Hemp Board

"Hemp is of first necessity to the wealth and protection of the country."
Thomas Jefferson, (3rd President of the USA, 1743-1826)

Hemp is used in the same way as straw and wood fibres in MDF. The inner core of the hemp, as opposed to the more expensive outer fibres, is used. Hemp is one of the faster-growing biomass plants known and can reach heights of up to 20 feet. It produces incredibly strong fibres – seven times stronger than cotton – that can be made into cloth. It was used to make the sails that powered European explorers across the world. Now China (currently one of the world's top hemp growers) has the chance to conquer the globe with it again!

Hempboard is an amazing product because the board is highly naturally fire retardant and moisture resistant, so no toxic chemical additives are necessary. It is important that we use more natural materials such as hempboard that have such useful characteristics. The more materials we use that reduce the need for using man-made chemicals, the better for us all.

Hemp grows anywhere and requires no herbicides or pesticides. It is biodegradable and renewable. An acre of hemp can produce the same amount of paper as 4 acres of wood. And because hemp's roots anchor down to 6 feet, it is of great benefit to areas of land where soil erosion might have been a problem.

The paper industry offers even greater possibilities. As an industry it amounts to over $1,000,000,000 a year, and of that, eighty per cent is imported. But hemp can produce every grade of paper, and government figures estimate that 10,000 acres devoted to hemp will produce as much paper as 40,000 acres of average pulp land.

"Why use up the forests which were centuries in the making and the mines which required ages to lay down, if we can get the equivalent of forest and mineral products in the annual growth of the fields?"
Henry Ford

Hemp has been grown and manufactured worldwide for at least 10,000 years and is one of England's oldest crops. Places like Hempton, Hemel Hempstead, Hempbridge, and Hempholme are all named after the hemp once grown there. It was such an important crop during the reign of Elizabeth I that fines of five gold sovereigns were given to farmers who wouldn't grow it.

Hemp was used for ship rigging, sails, uniforms, and lamp oil – as well as literally thousands of other products. This is eloquent testimony to the importance of hemp to England's maritime supremacy at the time. A heritage like that makes it amazing that it's still illegal to grow hemp in the US, but the plant is grown in Canada, China, the UK, France, Germany and many other countries and its future looks assured.

Recycled Plastic

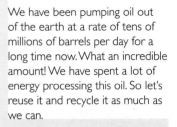

These toilet doors were made using recycled plastic. They have lots of interesting patterns and colours. ▼

We have been pumping oil out of the earth at a rate of tens of millions of barrels per day for a long time now. What an incredible amount! We have spent a lot of energy processing this oil. So let's reuse it and recycle it as much as we can.

I certainly don't mean that we should be pumping all the oil we can out of the ground. I mean that we should make use of what is already here – from plastic bottles, blue water pipes and yellow gas pipes, to office cups and packaging. These and many other plastics and materials can be recycled in many different ways.

Recycling plastic uses between 50 and 70% of the energy that would be used to create the product from virgin material. It does not require the pumping of more oil from the earth – and all the consequences associated with that. Furthermore, you are reusing materials and saving space in landfill and pollution from incinerators. When plastic is burned in an incinerator it does not just disappear. It creates toxic emissions and an incredibly toxic ash which still has to be landfilled.

Smile Plastics in the UK make boards using all sorts of interesting materials – such as corrugated transparent roofing with crushed shards of CDs scattered throughout. They have just brought out a new plastic sheet made of old coffee cups from dispensers mixed with used coffee grounds. These plastic sheets are very colourful and can be used on their own or as feature panels to add colour and design to furniture. They are great for use outdoors – such as for children's playgrounds or outdoor sheds.

It is becoming increasingly expensive to take waste to landfill. But by recycling rubbish, you can get money from the waste instead of having to pay to throw it away. Previously, companies did not have any incentive for recycling their rubbish unless they really understood the importance of caring for their environment. But it now undeniably makes economic sense to recycle.

EcoSheet laminated with wood at the edges ▼

The first manmade plastic was created by Alexander Parkes, who demonstrated it in public for the first time at the 1862 Great International Exhibition in London. The material was called Parkesine and was an organic material derived from cellulose. So plastic made from plants is nothing new. If we could do it in 1862, imagine what we are capable of now – or would have been, had we carried on the research... Let's catch up! Years later in 1950, the world was using 5 million tonnes of plastic – a figure which had increased to 100 million in 2001.

Packaging is the largest use of plastics in the UK, representing a 35% chunk. And at 23%, building and construction represents the next largest proportion. So it is great that plastics are being recycled into board that can be used in the construction of houses and fitted furniture.

There are now around 50 different groups of plastics, comprising hundreds of different varieties. All types of plastic are recyclable – but unfortunately not all types are currently collected or recycled by local councils. I hope that this becomes a priority soon. Then we will be able to benefit from an even more spectacular variety of boards.

A material called EcoSheet it is made from a huge range of different plastics combined including bubble gum. It makes you wonder why we put that stuff in our mouths!

The amount of plastic waste generated annually in the UK is estimated to be nearly 3 million tonnes.

Plastic bags and other plastic garbage thrown into the ocean kill as many as 1 million sea creatures every year.

According to a 2001 Environment Agency report, 80% of post-consumer plastic waste is sent to landfill, 8% is incinerated and only 7% is recycled.

Recycling a single plastic bottle can conserve enough energy to light a 60W bulb for up to 6 hours.

It takes 450 years just for one plastic bottle to break down in the ground.

Only 3-5% of plastic bottles are currently recycled in Europe.

56% of plastic is used in packaging, three quarters of which is from domestic households.

57% of litter found on beaches in 2003 was plastic in origin.

It takes about 25 recycled plastic drinks bottles to make one fleece jacket.

Americans use 4 million plastic bottles every hour – yet only 1 bottle out of 4 is recycled.

One tonne of plastic is equivalent to 20,000 two-litre drinks bottles.

Over 46,000 pieces of plastic debris float on every square mile of ocean.

2.2.134

Glass

Bottle Alley in Yorkshire is a company run by Alan Ashbee that takes unwanted glass bottles from people and turns them into beautiful glass panels suitable for use as worktops, splash-backs and many other things. The panels look beautiful in fitted furniture with lights behind them – or as glass tops to protect the furniture. The glass comes mainly from two recycling charities. One is called Bottle Rescue, which employs people with learning difficulties. The other is a social enterprise called Nicholas Fields (who also employ people with learning difficulties, including one of Alan's children). Nicholas Fields staff cycle around picking up bottles from Yorkshire pubs.

The white and green top we have used on the Milo table pictured is made of Newcastle Ale and Gordon's Gin bottles. Alan is proud that their panels use no additives or colourings with their glass making it purer and more natural because they are not needing to add extra chemicals into the process. The glass is fused together and not set in resin – which is again saving on virgin material.

A Milo table made of strawboard with a recycled glass top. Made by Bottle Alley Glass. ▼

Standard Materials

◄ *90% of materials use formaldehyde based glues*

A lot of people these days experience chronic illness – and I believe a lot of this illness is due to chemicals in the environment and in our homes that wreak havoc on the immune system. We don't have to have these. We can choose better, safer materials – and these days, with so many people providing natural and sustainable products, we have a great choice.

In the US, formaldehyde is not banned, but it has been regulated – meaning that it can only be used for certain things and in certain quantities. Formaldehyde is used to bind the sawdust fibres together in MDF, chipboard and plywood boards – which together make up the major construction material in hotels, bars, offices, public buildings and homes.

Some 120,000 emergency trailers were built and provided by the Federal Emergency Management Agency during hurricane Katrina to people who had lost their homes – but the government has now banned them from ever being used for long term housing again. Within months of people living in the trailers, residents had begun complaining about breathing problems and burning eyes, noses and throats. Federal officials later discovered that formaldehyde – which can cause nasal cancer, aggravates respiratory problems and may be linked to leukaemia – was present in many of these housing units in amounts that exceeded federal limits. Scientists have since concluded that the high levels of formaldehyde found in the trailers probably resulted from cheap wood and poor ventilation.

Formaldehyde is considered a human carcinogen, or cancer-causing substance, by the International Agency for Research on Cancer and a probable human carcinogen by the US Environmental Protection Agency. Not the kind of thing you want to be near to. We should avoid contact as much as possible by using low- or non-formaldehyde MDF, or innovative materials that are totally natural. For example, I have discovered a glue made in America, from soya flour. It contains no formaldehyde, has low VOCs (volatile organic compounds) and is cheaper than MDI (which is the next best currently available alternative to formaldehyde glue).

In general, I don't think that using a food crop for anything other than food is a good idea – unless there is nothing else that will do it or it is a by-product of food production. But this product shows that if you can use soya to make glue, you can surely also use other natural plant- or animal-based materials. One of my biggest missions is to help bring about a fibreboard which uses a completely natural glue.

Paints are also a cocktail of chemicals, and we have no idea of the exact effect they have on our bodies. Companies such as Auro, Earthborne, and Nutshell make paints that use mostly or totally natural materials. In Auro's case, organically-grown boiled linseed oil is used as the main binding resin in the paint. Growing this actively takes up CO_2 instead of producing it.

Auro's factory uses solar energy and wind power to reduce emissions. In fact Auro are the only paint manufacturer to be accredited as CO_2 neutral – achieving their balance through the Climate Neutral Group. Auro's water-based products contain no biocides, so have become the standard for hypoallergenic and child-friendly environments. They are perfect for cots and toys and carry EU certification.

Auro's new flagship product – 328 Airfresh paint – actively neutralises smells and pollutants in a room and has been certified to degrade formaldehyde by 95% after just 2 hours of application. Auro's founder Dr Herman Fischer became convinced that only by using naturally occurring materials exclusively could we avoid the risk of toxic contamination from the products of synthetic chemistry.

▲ *Natural paints use linseed resins and plant-based pigments and so are non-toxic.*

Furniture for the Future by Tristan Titeux

Wood

Approximately 80% of timber from the Brazilian Amazon is logged illegally.

Avoid products made with hardwoods that are likely to originate from the rainforest. If you are unsure, buy products or specify a company that uses British, European and American wood. And don't buy any wood or product that is not FSC-certified.

In 2002 alone, an area of Amazon rainforest the size of Belgium was deforested.

Plywood (other than the cheapest type, which uses softwood) will most likely be made using tropical wood from rainforest trees – so for that reason I think FSC-certified MDF is best for furniture. The eco-MDF uses only 2-3 % glue, compared to 12-15 % for the traditional MDF. MDF wood is grown in the UK too, reducing transport miles. Birch and beech ply is also fine if it is made from FSC-certified trees grown in Europe.

One wood to avoid totally is a mahogany from Asia called *Dipterocarpus spp* or Keruing. This name is given to around 70 commercially-harvested timbers from the mahogany family, half of which are listed by the IUCN (International Union for Conservation of Nature) as 'critically endangered' or 'endangered'.

In 2003 an estimated 88% of logging in Indonesia was illegal.

Bandsaw in an illegal logging factory in the Pacific rainforest. ▼

Wenge – an exotic hardwood that is currently in vogue – does not have an FSC alternative and is listed as vulnerable, as is African walnut, and there are many other woods listed as vulnerable, endangered or critically endangered. By insisting that suppliers prove that their wood is FSC-certified you will be going a long way towards preventing the loss of cultures and habitats in South America due to illegal logging.

The lack of governance and law enforcement means that murder, violence, slavery and the illegal occupancy of public land are widespread in the Amazon. The Amazon basin supports almost half of all known land based species. It also has one of the world's highest rates of forest destruction – and the pace is increasing.

In Indonesia (where a lot of tropical wood is sourced from the rainforest), at least 50 million indigenous people depend on the forests. The destruction of these forests goes hand in hand with corruption and human rights abuses.

In Malaysia, production capacity in plywood and furniture mills exceeds the volume of timber actually available from the country's forests. As a result, Sahah in Borneo, once the centre of the timber industry in Malaysia, has virtually run out of raw materials. Despite legislation in both countries banning the transportation of round logs from Indonesia to Malaysia, estimates suggest that a significant proportion of the logs needed by Sarawak's processing industry are smuggled illegally from Indonesia. Malaysian timber is increasingly being certified by the Malaysian Timber Certification Council. But among other failings, this certification scheme does not recognise the land rights of indigenous communities or offer sufficient protection for high conservation value forests.

2.3

MY PIONEERING FITTED FURNITURE PROJECTS

What makes Custom Carpentry's fitted furniture pioneering is that we use eco-friendly materials that are not normally found in fitted furniture together with other unusual natural materials. We combine these with green and ethical business practices that are perhaps unique in the world of fitted furniture.

"Humankind has not woven the web of life. We are but one thread within it. Whatever we do to the web, we do to ourselves. All things are bound together. All things connect."
Chief Seattle (1855)

I am not a follower but a leader – a very ambitious person driven by a strong passion to help others. Everything at Custom Carpentry – from our ethical banking, green electricity, office reuse and recycling policies, our Custom Carpentry chickens that sleep on shredded office paper, eat our organic lunch food scraps and produce eggs to power our minds and bodies – all these things help to clarify our place and responsibility on earth: it helps to remind us every day as we work that we are part of a whole ecosystem.

The intelligent design that underwrites our eco-furniture means our products can be used and reused by our customers and ultimately, disposed of safely at the end of their useful life, although my aim is to never have a disposal point – what I call a 'dead end point' – but instead, for our furniture to return to the earth as compost and to fuel the growth of other materials. All this contributes to the greenest fitted furniture company around today.

One of our free-range Custom Carpentry hens▶

These are just the early stages for us. We are constantly looking for greener, more thoughtful and better ways to run our company: our van can run on recycled old chip oil (as can any diesel van) and the more eco-resources become available, the more Custom Carpentry will be at the cutting-edge, pushing the barriers of what is possible, innovating, and helping our clients to have confidence in the 'green option'.

Furniture for the Future by Tristan Titeux

The Stram Straw Project

Floating shelves made from Stramit. ▼

I love wood and trees and I love wooden houses, but when I discovered strawbale building I was hooked by the idea that you could make a house very quickly, simply and cheaply by using whole strawbales. I will use straw bales when I build my ultimate home to show how simple, healthy, modern and beautiful it can be.

I love the idea that straw comes from the land, grows each year from seed and so is a renewable resource, and is a simple and a natural product. When I started looking into materials that I could use to improve our eco-fitted furniture range at Custom Carpentry, I came across strawboard. I was inspired by the idea of using it in our fitted furniture, but the sad thing was that no one was making strawboard in the UK. After almost losing hope on finding any straw-based materials for my furniture, I came across an insulating material made by Stramit, which is made in the UK. What really exited me was that no glue is used to hold the straw fibres together, just high pressure.

To my knowledge, this is the first time that anyone has used Stramit to make fitted furniture. We used the strawboard to make floating shelves in two alcoves of a living room. We also replaced the fireplace surround which was not very nice nor in keeping with the whole design. I really didn't know what to expect of this strawboard as we had never used it before, but I was determined to make it work. We left the front of the shelving exposed so that people can see the end-grain of the straw – and, like an 'honesty window in a strawbale house that exposes the bales to prove the house is really made of straw – we wanted the straw in our shelving to show. This could be painted over and covered-up if a completely clean look is required, but I like the idea of having rough and contrasting smooth edges.

▲ *Close-up of Stramit shelf showing compressed strawboard raw edge.*

We made a larger straw shelf at the bottom for a DVD play or Skybox, and mounted the TV on the wall to save surface space. We hid wires for the TV and equipment behind 4mm thick hardboard. We also used hardboard to cover wires on both sides for the electric lights.

I like to emphasise the qualities of light in my designs: it brings a storage unit to life and makes it beautiful. The lights used in this shelving unit are low-powered 16 watts per meter and are low voltage, so could run directly off a 12v system of batteries running on solar power. The lights are LEDs (light emitting diodes) and are commonly used for lighting. They consume very little electricity, are long lasting and therefore can be considered to be eco-friendly compared to halogen lighting.

Recycled plastic with low-wattage LED light strip behind bring interesting qualities to the shelving unit. ▼

In front of the lighting we used recycled plastic sheeting from Smile Plastics. The sheet we used was made from crushed CDs suspended in recycled office water bottles. I added this to demonstrate the interesting qualities of low voltage lighting and recycled plastic, although the plastic was not as blue and transparent as I was hoping for.

The overall design is simple, clean, modern and will complement any style and so pass the test of time. It can be repainted again and again with no degradation of the quality of the original piece. We tested different paints and varnishes from Biofa white paint to Auro's paint, varnish and oil. Incidentally, Auro Paints also make a cleaner for brushes that is natural and made from orange oil. I like it because it is made from renewable resources: natural plant based materials and not petro-chemicals. We also used powdered filler by Auro to fill any holes and cracks.

To blend the shelves into the existing wall we used a water-based flexible filler that uses reusable outer packaging from Geocel called ecoSEAL, and lastly we used water-based gap-filling glue to bond different materials if needed. The last two are still petrol-based but are VOC free, so better for the user and the environment.

Furniture for the Future by Tristan Titeux

At the bottom of the shelves between the floor and the first shelves on each side there is a removable panel to conceal the transformer for the lights so that if it goes wrong it can easily be replaced. It also conceals the plugs and plug sockets on each side, which hides ugly wires but leaves them accessible for repair. The panel is made of hardboard and is doubled in thickness to make it extra stiff. Hardboard is a natural material because it just uses wood fibres compressed to a very high pressure mixed with water. All the water escapes through a mesh leaving a web-like texture on one side and a totally smooth surface on the other. It is natural because it uses no glue at all in the process. The future is already here! Although hardboard is a common material in the UK building industry, a lot of it is imported, particularly from Russia. This does not please me, but the fact that it is a totally healthy, natural organic and compostable material is exciting. I will keep looking for a British source if one exists and if not, promote the fact that we need one.

▲ EcoSeal has a reusable outer casing.

At the end of its useful life the straw furniture can be composted or disposed of in the ground with minimal effect on the environment, as after removing the flexible filler, all that is left is natural and non-toxic. If you have chickens or other farm animals, or you have a vegetable garden that you want to mulch, you can easily pull out the straw from the shelving and reuse it as bedding. So, although not yet perfect, it is pretty close to perfection. That really excites me! I feel inspired by the opportunity that nature has given me to showcase her great materials.

To find out more details about strawboard, type 'strawboard' into YouTube and you will see a lot more about Stram Straw. Also check out my blog at www.customcarpentry.co.uk/blog

Flexi-Straw:
The home-office, multi-purpose general storage unit or wardrobe

As with the Stram Straw project, the key material is straw, bonded with non-formaldehyde MDI glue: an improvement on formaldehyde-based glues but still derived from petroleum, so I am trying to highlight the fact that we need to find alternative glues or ideally, technologies using no glues and local materials. Unfortunately, this board is imported from China as it is not available in Europe: my aim in using it is to show the potential in using a waste material that is a by-product of producing grain. If I can show in the short term that it is possible to use it as a furniture-building material and if I can raise awareness of the benefits of using 'waste' in this way, then I will be helping to encourage the use of more varied materials rather than just relying on wood, with all the environmental issues that creates.

The Flexi-Straw storage cupboard is very special: it is designed to be beautiful, simple, flexible, multi-use and therefore has an extended useful life, which makes it a very sustainable furniture option. Its design is elegant, with long straight doors, all in white which reflects light and makes the room bright and healthy, and complements any other colour or texture. This particular unit shown in the photograph was designed initially to fit around an existing fish tank, so instead of buying a new one specially, we reused the existing one instead of getting rid of it. Above the fish tank is a push-up shelf on hinges to allow easy access to the top of the fish tank for cleaning and servicing. The fishtank was featured in the centre of the unit to make it the main point of focus.

◀ *Close-up showing fishtank in place and oiled strawboard frame.*

If a client wants to change the use of this unit and turn it into an office it is possible to just take out the tank, remove the framing panel that covers the front of the tank (which is simply held in place with magnets) and use the space for a computer monitor. There is a built-in shelf for a keyboard that pulls out and is just the right height for typing, and at the end of the working day, the keyboard shelf can be pushed back in and the doors closed.

▲ *The pull-out shelf is a great way to instantly extend your space.*

The wires for the computer and screen can be plugged directly into an extension socket that is already in place behind the pull-out keyboard, so no major reconfiguration is needed. Electrical points that were also used for the fishtank are right there where you need them. Holes are also drilled in the shelves for the wires to pass through. The computer tower can fit anywhere below the keyboard shelf, so everything is neatly in one area.

The TV can be mounted in the unit if the
▼ *fishtank is no longer wanted.*

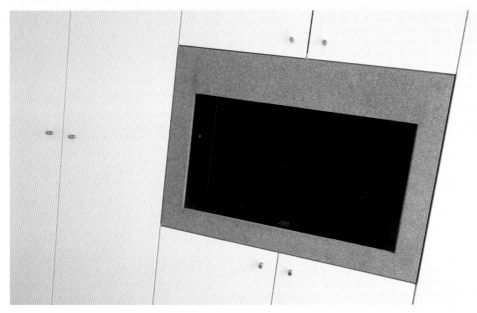

If at a later date you want to use the room as a TV room with an entertainment unit you can replace the computer monitor with the TV and either leave the strawboard frame around or not, and again all holes and sockets are available for the electrics, the DVD etc. Or, if you don't want a TV, that central section could be used to display a beautiful sculpture or piece of art, or you could put a mirror in the back, and add some glass shelves. It is possible to easily modify that space with very little skill.

Inside the cupboard itself, every shelf can either be moved up or down or removed altogether to make bigger spaces between the shelves. This means that the unit is totally adaptable. The cupboard also has different depths and widths, because it was built spanning 2 different width alcoves and a chimney breast, so it has deeper sections where the alcoves are, which in this case were fitted with hanging rails for hanging clothes.

▲ Screw holes are left clear for ease of deconstruction, panels are made of straw instead of wood

If you wanted that space as a utility storage area for really large items you could easily remove the rails and fit some new shelves on the existing adjustable peg holes that are already drilled in the side uprights of the wardrobe ready to fit your shelves.

And at the end of all that if you still don't want or need the cupboard anymore it can easily be taken apart because we used no glue to put it together and we left all screw holes exposed so that you can simply unscrew the unit without damaging the individual planks, making it possible to actually rebuild it somewhere else, or it can be used to make other fitted or freestanding furniture, shelving etc.

Or if none of this works then you can send it to your recycling centre for recycling. It would be a real service to the community if there were places in every town and city where people could donate any wood or materials that are no longer wanted, where the materials could be graded according to their size and usability, so that other people could select materials that they can reuse, instead of using new materials which are more expensive to the wallet and to the environment.

The Flexi-Straw cupboard is designed to be healthy within the home: we painted the whole of the front with a VOC-free paint, which dries quickly and doesn't smell. We also used Auro Hard Oil that is made of totally natural materials such as orange oil, linseed oil, castor and sunflower oil on the outside central piece so you can see the texture and grain of the strawboard. We left one section completely untreated to see how it would look and stand the test of time. We used Auro powdered filler where needed: it is made from chalk, a natural material that requires very little processing. A flexible eco-filler was also used to join and blend the cupboard into the existing walls and make them look seamless.

Here you can see the strawboard frame contrasting nicely with the painted surface and the minimal handles. ▼

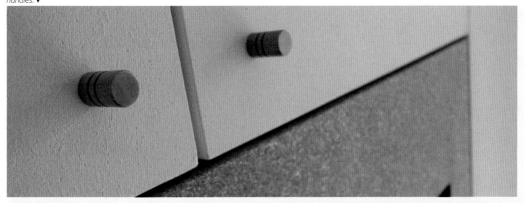

You can see how much stainless steel small, minimalist handles save compared to this standard handle. ▼

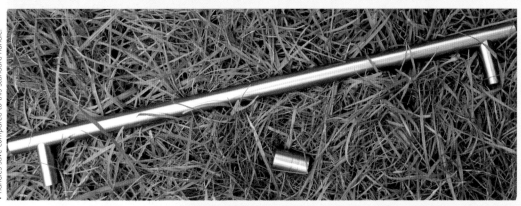

The cupboard is also designed to use minimal amounts of metal: we could have used wooden handles, but the importance of a clean, contemporary design is also a key factor, and I really love the contrast of metal and natural materials. When contrasting materials are used together it highlights their individual qualities. I choose small handles because they use 15 times less material that the usual 28cm long bar handle. They are minimalist in design and fit perfectly with the design of the simple doors. Stainless steel is very long lasting, is made of around 60% recycled material and is totally recyclable and does not degrade in quality. It is inert and non-polluting if it reaches landfill – so again, it is a good eco-option.

Because stainless steel is very corrosion-resistant, this means it will last a long time outdoors, but indoors, in theory it will last forever. When the unit is no longer required, the handles can just be taken off and reused, sold or recycled. Due to the hardness of the metal, the thread will not break like an aluminium or softer steel one might, therefore aiding its longevity and therefore sustainability. To me, stainless steel used in this way looks beautiful: it has a really nice raw quality, is exciting to look at and feel.

▲ *Straw bales, the by-product of grain production have many and varied uses, not least in eco-fitted furniture. © Stefan Lubo www.stefanlubo.com*

There is plenty of straw in the UK: over 11 million tonnes per year is produced, but approximatedly 2 million tonnes of it is wasted. Straw has been used in building for a long time – traditionally, mixed with mud to make cob walls for houses, and more recently used as whole straw bales (rectangular) to create walls which are then clad with clay or lime plasters. It is an amazing natural material. I love it.

The 'Marco' Project:

Children's fitted furniture

The 'Marco' project was designed specifically with children in mind and therefore it was imperative that all materials and paints used didn't harm the health of the child in any way. In one corner of the room where this fitted furniture was to be installed, there was an alcove, which we used for floating shelves that were made to look like they just grew out of the wall!

For this project I chose to use a hollow core board that is made with cardboard on the inside in a honeycomb pattern for strength. Selecting this material means that less precious wood has been used: instead this material replaces the wood component with a recycled paper product made from pulp that uses less glue to hold the wood fibres together than if it had been made from solid MDF. It was important to minimise any petrochemical-derived glues that contain formaldehyde in this project.

To deal with the formaldehyde and to stop it escaping out of the glue we used a flexible filler to seal it to the wall, which also makes the end result look very neat. The Geocel flexible filler we use is waterbased and low in VOCs, and comes in reusable packaging. To seal-in the MDF or chipboard totally to avoid formaldehyde off-gassing we used a special product called 'MDF passifier' which effectively seals the shelves. We then painted them with waterbased VOC-free eco paints.

This cardboard inner reduces the amount of raw wood and glue needed in the project. ▼

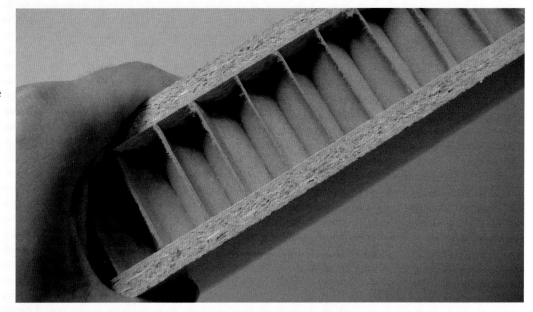

White or light colours are always a good idea for children's furniture and rooms because of their light reflective qualities, making spaces seem bigger, brighter and more relaxing for the mind compared with darker colours. As light colours reflect the light, it also means less electricity is needed.

Clean alcove wardrobes. ▼

On the other side of the chimney-breast in the right alcove I designed a wardrobe with floor to ceiling doors that make the room look higher-ceilinged and give clean, simple and modern lines. I used a special MDF wood called 'Medite Ecologique' which contains no formaldehyde at all and is made of an MDI glue, which is inert. Unfortunately, it is still derived from fossil fuel and is polluting to produce and energy intensive, but it is currently the best option we have.

The design of the wardrobe is eminently flexible: it has adjustable shelves and the hanging rails can easily be adapted to a growing child's needs. It also has the small stainless steel handles described previously, because they use less resources and are aesthetically pleasing. The unit is put together using no glue and all screws have been left discretely hidden but exposed so that it can be taken apart easily. The inside of the wardrobe was painted with AURO paint made of natural materials, but because it has a tendency to yellow slightly we used a water based paint on the outside which stays perfectly white.

Children's wardrobe with removable hanging rails and adjustable shelves. ▼

Contemporary Eco-fitted TV Unit

This living room storage cupboard was designed after taking into account the client's own ideas and needs. I spent a lot of time finding out exactly what she wanted to use the furniture for and how she wanted it to look. We did many Skype sessions together where I could share my computer screen with her and discuss and amend the 3D drawings. Planning and comprehensive consulting is essential to getting a unit that the customer is totally delighted with and will keep for as long as possible, rather than getting bored of it and replacing it every few years.

I find this process incredibly satisfying and love it when both client and designer get that "YES!" feeling where you both know it is perfect! As I don't get involved in construction anymore this is where I do my constructing: on the computer and with customers. I enjoy the interaction with them: I love to please and this is a way I can do so.

This unit was built using many of the previously-mentioned techniques in this chapter. There are a few things that are different that I want to point out. The inside of this unit is made using a pre-finished chipboard material which uses up to 40% less recycled wood and it is made in the UK, which makes it a more sustainable product.

Eco-furniture does not have to look any different to more traditionally-produced products, but it is remarkable because it is ethically-sound and therefore you can use it with a clear conscience. ▶

All the outside visible surfaces and the doors where made using Medite Ecologique which is a formaldehyde-free alternative to MDF. It is painted with an eco-paint sold by Nutshell Paints and is made using non-petrochemical ingredients. Hand painted furniture is more sustainable than spray-painted furniture, because it can be easily repaired, patched up or completely repainted whereas sprayed, veneered or melamine-coated finishes once damaged are either irreparable or difficult to do so.

A close-up of one of the shelving niches in this eco-fitted TV unit, which being hand-built in the UK supports local craftsmen and the local ▼ economy.

▲ *Top-routed handles minimise raw materials and add to the minimal design.*

Clever use of LED lighting makes the unit almost look as if it is hovering. ▶

The unit uses low wattage and low voltage LEDs because they use less energy and look amazing: the glow is just magical, and they last 'forever' unlike halogen bulbs that are also fiddly to change. If you have a 12V solar panel system you can run these lights from it as they are 12V too, so you don't need a step-down transformer which wastes energy. I believe low voltage systems will be much more common in the future. So many of our electronic goods use low voltage: your TV, radio, bedside clock...

The handles are routed-out to the top and bottom edge of the doors which adds to the minimal design and also uses less materials such as the stainless steel that would normally be used for door handles, therefore using less precious resources.

Furniture for the Future by Tristan Titeux

The Milo Series and the ReCut Series

When we build our fitted furniture, there is inevitably a lot of waste created, and when we fit furniture we sometimes have to take out unwanted furniture from people's houses because it is poorly built, ugly or does not serve a purpose any more. I hate to see all this material go to waste and I end up hoarding it because I just can't bear to throw it away. So in 2011, I decided to create the ReCut Series – and the first piece we produced was a small coffee table called Milo.

Tristan Titeux amongst his ReCut Series, made from waste off-cuts. ▼

The Milo table uses small pieces of off-cut material that are no good for anything else. These are glued together with an eco-friendly glue made from renewable plant-based materials, and is sanded smooth on the outside surfaces then oiled with a natural oil. In contrast, the Milo is left totally uneven and rough underneath. I really like the idea of rough and smooth edges contrasting together, but also I hope it will make people look at the Milo more closely, to compare the rough and smooth; to see the real materials that have gone into making the piece and to and think about its origins more deeply.

Milo is made in layers that are visible to encourage people to see all the different materials that have gone into its making. As well as looking beautiful – a little like those bottles filled with sand that we made when we were little – I hope that people will become interested in the materials as they are: all exposed looking interesting and beautiful.

I want people to question where the materials they use in their homes come from and to think about the trees that have been cut down to create them: were they from the rainforests of the world, or were they from a sustainably managed forest, and what is the difference? Has the wood used in a particular product come via illegal logging with corrupt officials turning a blind eye to the consequent deforestation? Is the product made from trees that are hundreds of years old, whether that be in the Amazon, Canada or Russia? Has making the product destroyed natural irreplaceable resources? Are indigenous people killed to get to the trees on their land? Is the product made with glue? How is the glue made? Is it a petrochemical glue? How much pollution is created in the manufacture of the product? Are workers in danger whilst producing the raw materials to make it? What wars and crimes are created because of the oil needed to produce and ship these products? How much blood has been shed to create it? These are incredibly complex questions and they all relate to the purchase of just one piece of furniture.

I really want people to look at their furniture and see past it to the world behind it: to see that things don't just happen by magic and that usually someone or something suffers. Nothing is free, it is all borrowed from someone or something else. If we have something for free it is because someone or something else has given it to us, and the more someone has, the less someone else has. That is the law of nature, no need to think too hard about it, if you take something out of one place, you leave a vacuum that needs to be filled.

So I just want to use waste and do something positive with it – to make something practical and beautiful, that people will want to keep forever.

To learn more about the Milo series use these keywords for an online search: 'Milo Tristan Titeux'

The Milo table upside-down, where you can see the different layers. ▼

Furniture for the Future by Tristan Titeux

My customer wanted to turn her old wardrobe into a bedside table because she was very attached to it as it saved her life when her whole chimney fell through the roof and bedroom ceiling: the old wardrobe bore the brunt of the damage, stopping the masonry from falling on her.

I showed her the Milo Table brochure that I carry everywhere with me and she agreed that would be a great way to reconstruct her damaged wardrobe. The table was consequently made, and as you can see, it makes a stylish addition to her room.

Bespoke Milo Tables

The table was varnished on the top and sides, but left rough and unfinished on the inside, giving an interesting contrast. On the outside and inside of the legs, you can see the original blue of the wardrobe doors.

I love the idea of bringing something back to life like this, rather than throwing it away.

◄ *This bespoke Milo bedside table was made from a client's old wardrobe*

Straw Exhibition at SCIN Architectural Gallery

SCIN is a new materials showroom and art gallery on four floors in London's Old Street. It opened in 2012 to promote innovative materials and technologies to local architects and designers, and they are particularly interested in using ecological materials. In January 2012 on one of their floors they held a themed exhibition using straw. The gallery found my Stram Straw blogs and research on the internet, and invited me to take part and make some shelves especially for the exhibition. I designed a variety of straw shelving made with from Stramit Strawboard and Flexi Straw strawboard.

The Stram Straw shelf we made was raw and unfinished, with nothing to cover-up the edges – in fact I wanted to show the straw all ruffled-up, enabling people to see the compacted straw with no glue. I then designed another shelf using the same material but painted white with Nutshell eco-paints and the ends were finished off with hardboard, which is just compacted wood fibre with no glue.

▲ *This is the Stram Straw shelf. I love its simplicity and rawness, contrasting with the modern white background.*

Collection of straw shelves designed by Tristan Titeux ▶

Furniture for the Future by Tristan Titeux

▲ This strawboard floating shelf was oiled with an Auro natural oil and features a recycled plastic strip.

The other shelves were made from glued strawboard and I had some left-over recycled CD plastic so used that as a feature. Another shelf featured a strip of recycled glass from Bottle Alley Glass.

Untreated strawboard with recycled glass strip lit with LEDs. ▼

Behind The Scenes at Custom Carpentry

I started Custom Carpentry in 2003. I inherited the name from a customer I was working with: her husband had passed away and had been using the name for over 15 years. She very kindly let me have the name, and also gave me some of his tools. I run a small team of 6 people who I care about very much. I am very loyal and fair but I expect a lot in return. I don't ask anyone to do anything I would not do myself!

I got into carpentry because I wanted to go and live in France in the countryside and build my own house, plant a garden and keep animals. I did a variety of courses to help me including cider making, strawbale building, permaculture, blacksmithing, renewable energy, basket making, pottery and, more to the point, a two-year carpentry course. My dream of a house in France is on hold right now, as I'm currently raising my family and running Custom Carpentry in Notting Hill, London.

Custom Carpentry is a cutting-edge business: we are not afraid to experiment with new materials but what else is it that makes us an exceptional company? Well, it is great to make fitted furniture with eco-friendly materials, but to be a truly sustainable fitted furniture company, the philosophy must run all the way through the business. So, the other practical things we do make a big difference: we have been using renewable electricity from the sun and the wind since 2003 from Good Energy. It feels great to know that when we use an electric saw, we are not creating carbon emissions in the process.

In the office we use recycled paper so we know that trees are not being unnecessarily cut down. We print on both sides of the paper thereby reducing paper use by half, and we reuse other scraps of paper for note-taking where possible. Once that paper has been totally used we then shred it into tiny pieces and use it as bedding for our chickens. Then, once it has been used as bedding, it goes in the compost bin and eventually back into the earth. Altogether a very satisfying experience for us! All cardboard boxes also get composted or used to package and protect our products. Our work clothes are sourced from Fair Trade manufacturers, our T-shirts are unbleached organic cotton, thereby saving tons of nasty chemicals. Our fleece jackets are 100% recycled made from 75 plastic water bottles. We recycle food waste via our chickens! As well as feeding them organically grown grain, the leftovers from our lunches go to the chickens and in return, we get lovely eggs.

We bank ethically too. I have had an account with The Cooperative Bank for over 10 years and our business account is also with them. It is true that their website and internet banking leaves a lot to be desired, but I persevere because I know our money will not go towards buying weapons and nuclear energy. I am voting with my money and saying that I don't want war. And finally, at night I turn off all our electrical equipment, computers and lights.

> Don't get me wrong: I love nuclear energy! It's just that I prefer fusion to fission. And it just so happens that there's an enormous fusion reactor safely banked a few million miles from us. It delivers more than we could ever use in just about 8 minutes. And it's wireless!
>
> - William McDonough – Fortune Brainstorm Conference, 2006

APPENDICES

3.1

WHERE'S MILO?

The recycled table that's going places

Furniture for the Future by Tristan Titeux

#wheresMilo © Tristan Titeux

Furniture for the Future by Tristan Titeux

13

14

15

16

www.tristantiteux.com

3.1.167

1. Milo on a lovely beach at Hartland Quay, Devon

2. Milo is having fun at the skatepark in Meanwhile Gardens, Westbourne Park, London

3. Milo visiting the team at Waste Watch to promote discussion about recycling and waste in schools

4. Milo with Robert Taylor, who wrote the children's comedy 'Chucklevision' and is now a media lawyer

5. Milo at the foot of what was the biggest and most important fort of World War 2 in the valley where I grew up in Belgium

6. Milo with Henri Hardy sculptor from Belgium who I have known since birth

7. Milo with my neighbour and Belgian sculptor Jos Van Vreeswijk

8. Milo with Sven from Po-Zu.com natural footwear

9. Milo with Goldie, international Drum & Bass DJ, music producer, graffiti and contemporary artist

10. Milo is with the Design and Technology department of Norbury Manor Business and Enterprise College for Girls, after a talk on eco-materials.

11. Milo with Stefan Lubo www.stefanlubo.com, the amazing photographer who took the photos of Milo for my brochure

12. Milo with Dony (Anthony Schiepers), my friend from primary school, a musician who crashed his car and spent the repair money on this £1200 guitar

13. Milo in Torilla, a contemporary home built in 1934 in Hatfield, UK

14. Milo with Satish Kumar, Editor of Resurgence & The Ecologist magazine. He walked on an 8000 mile journey from India to America with no money to deliver a message of peace to the four leaders of the nuclear nations of that time

15. Milo with James Otter who makes eco-surfboards out of wood, finished with a plant-based resin

16. Milo with Gauthier Titeux and his family serving Belgian beers outside his Bed & Breakfast in the Belgian Ardennes

17. A bespoke Milo wine display unit made for the 'Naturally Chinese' restaurant in Kingston, London

ECODESIGNER HOME.COM

3.2

Ecodesingerhome.com is a new website concept by Tristan Titeux and is designed to be a one-stop shop where people can find out about some of the wonderful environmentally-friendly products that are now available to help you create a beautiful and healthful home.

Examples of some of the products available from ecodesignerhome.com ▼

Many of the products you have read about in this book are featured on the website: from clay plasters, eco paints, organic rugs, carpets, flooring, fitted furniture, upcycled furniture and natural local furniture to organic natural beds, bedding etc.

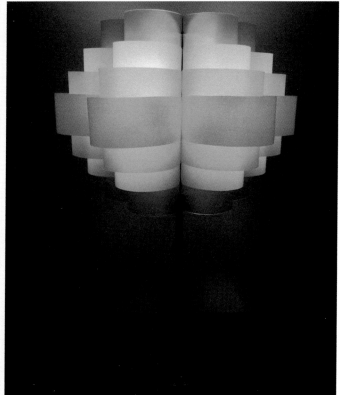

I am constantly on the look-out for fantastic new products that are recycled or upcycled or made from natural materials that are respectful of their impact on the planet. Ecodesignerhome.com will continue to expand and evolve to encompass a world of great design that will complement your home and your ethical values.

CHILDREN'S NATURAL BEDROOMS

3.3

EXAMPLES OF A CHILDREN'S ECO BEDROOM

CUSTOM CARPENTRY
Contemporary bespoke furniture

CHILDREN'S NATURAL BEDROOMS

Because your children's health is worth it

Natural Materials

Tel: 0800 458 9158 or 07770 431 55

www.CustomCapentry.co.uk/Eco

ECO

Passionate abou the PLANET

Do you have young children and are you concerned about all the pollutants we live with in our homes? Have you ever wondered what future we might be leaving our children, their children and their grand-children? We are living in interesting times: we have access to so much information and so many good products, but we often choose products for the wrong reasons; because they are cheap or in fashion. To make informed decisions, the questions we should be asking are: is this product made from sustainable materials; is it non-toxic; will it be healthy for my children?

I want to be part of making sure that our children grown healthy and have a great future. That is why I decided in 2010 to offer an eco-friendly option for children's fitted furniture. A child spends nearly half of their time sleeping in their bedroom, usually with closed windows. If we don't make good choices as parents, they will be breathing in the various indoor pollutants such as VOCs that are commonly present in bedding, curtains, carpets, toys, paints and furniture. Indoor air is many times more polluted than outdoor air. Sadly, cancer, asthma and other breathing illnesses and allergies are becoming increasingly common in children.

We now have the opportunity to make a difference and give them a better start, and my company can help design natural fitted furniture and provide other sustainable natural materials for your children's bedrooms. We specialise in formaldehyde-free fitted furniture painted with plant-based eco paint, natural organic carpets, wood flooring, clay plasters and natural wall paints, fairtrade organic hemp curtains and upholstery, freestanding furniture made from local sustainable wood hand made by British craftsmen to house plants that help clean the air.

Not only will you have the peace of mind that your child will be breathing in clean air, but you will be supporting ethical products that have been made with healthy people and a healthy planet in mind. Plus, you will be supporting local craftsmen and women and therefore the local economy, which is often by-passed for cheaper labour abroad. We have a choice: when we spend our money, why not spend it in a way that will make a great difference in the world and in your children's world?

SPREAD
THE WORD

For eco-fitted furniture visit www.CustomCarpentry.co.uk/eco

To create your dream eco-home visit www.EcoDesignerHome.com

To create a natural bedroom go to the blog on www.CustomCarpentry.co.uk and type 'natural bedrooms' in the search box.

If you know a school or business that wants Tristan to talk about eco-materials go to the blog on www.CustomCarpentry.co.uk and type 'talkworkshop' in the search box.

Visit Tristan's personal blog at www.TristanTiteux.com

To learn more about eco-materials go to www.TristanTiteux.com and click on the 'Eco-Friendly Materials' tab in the menu.

To learn more about Tristan's roots go to www.TristanTiteux.com and type 'The things that shaped me' in the search box.
Search Tristan Titeux in Google to find all his links. Here are some:

If you are interested in getting fitted furniture for your home, here are some tips to ask your fitted furniture company or carpenter: www.customcarpentry.co.uk/blog/the-7-biggest-mistakes-booklet

Connect With Tristan on Social Media

LinkedIn: www.linkedin.com/in/tristantiteux

Facebook
Personal: www.facebook.com/TristanTiteux
Custom Carpentry (Fitted Furniture): www.facebook.com/CustomCarpentryUK
Eco-Designer Home: www.facebook.com/EcoDesignerHome
Eco-Materials: www.facebook.com/EcoMaterialsUK
This Book: www.facebook.com/FurnitureForTheFuture

Twitter
Personal: twitter.com/TristanTiteux @TristanTiteux
Custom Carpentry (Fitted Furniture): twitter.com/FittedFurniture @FittedFurniture
Eco-Designer Home: twitter.com/EcoDesignerHome @EcoDesignerHome
Eco-Materials: twitter.com/EcoMaterialsUK @EcoMaterialsUK
This Book: twitter.com/FurnitureFTF

Pinterest: pinterest.com/tristantiteux/

YouTube: www.youtube.com/user/CustomCarpentryUK

Instagram: @TristanTiteux

Find me everywhere else by searching Tristan Titeux in Google

And this book has a website too at www.FurnitureForTheFuture.com or www.FurnitureForTheFuture.co.uk